W9-BLQ-194

COLLEGE

and

CAREER SUCCESS

for

STUDENTS

with

LEARNING

DISABILITIES

ROSLYN DOLBER

Printed on recyclable paper

VGM Career Horizons
a division of *NTC Publishing Group*
Lincolnwood, Illinois USA

Library of Congress Cataloging-in-Publication Data

Dolber, Roslyn.
  College and career success for students with learning disabilities
  / Roslyn Dolber.
      p.   cm.
  Includes bibliographical references and index.
  ISBN 0-8442-4479-1 (paperback)
    1. Learning disabled—Education (Higher)—United States.
  2. Learning disabled—Vocational guidance—United States.
  3. College choice—United States. 4. College student orientation—
  United States.   I. Title.
  LC4818.38.D65   1996
  371.91—dc20   96-3572
                                                        CIP

Published by VGM Career Horizons, a division of NTC Publishing Group.
4255 West Touhy Avenue,
Lincolnwood (Chicago), Illinois 60646-1975 U.S.A.
© 1996 by NTC Publishing Group. All rights reserved.
No part of this book may be reproduced, stored in a retrieval system,
or transmitted in any form or by any means,
electronic, mechanical, photocopying, recording or otherwise,
without the prior permission of NTC Publishing Group.
Manufactured in the United States of America.

6 7 8 9 0 VP 9 8 7 6 5 4 3 2 1

This book is for Matthew, who has helped me understand
the daily struggle and constant challenge for the learning disabled

Contents

Introduction

What Happens After High School?

If you are a high school junior or senior...get ready! You are close to graduation and time will seem to fly by. You may feel as though you can't wait to leave high school. At the same time, you may also be nervous about the changes that will take place. You are not alone. These are typical feelings for high school students getting ready for the next hurdle, which is often college.

The first step you will take as a college freshman is saying goodbye to everything that has been safe and familiar—family, good friends, routines—and moving on to:

- Experience new situations
- Meet new people
- Establish new goals

You will need to make lots of decisions and you will face many new responsibilities. You *can* handle it all—if you take it one step at a time!

Growing numbers of students with learning problems are attending colleges and universities across the nation. And more and more teenagers, along with their parents and high school counselors, are searching for programs that will be appropriate for their needs.

Education professionals say that there are more than one million high school students with learning disabilities nationwide, cutting across every class and segment of the population. If you have a learning disability, your life has already been marked with obstacles and frustrations.

When considering college, you will want to look for the educational environment that will best help you meet challenges and gain positive feelings about yourself and your ability to learn. The next job for you and for those who know you well is to assess your strengths as well as your shortcomings, and then match that information with a program that will support your needs.

Finding the appropriate college will be a challenge, but a rewarding one when the proper match is made. You should view this as a search for choosing a school or program that will fit all of your needs, including:

- Your educational needs

- Your social needs

- Your cultural needs

Every adolescent, learning disabled or not, can profit from an educational program beyond high school to:

- Prepare for careers

- Develop learning capabilities

- Become contributing members of the work force

Those who work in the field of **special education** report that the number of college students with learning disabilities continues to increase across college campuses. Colleges nationwide have acknowledged this population and have designed programs and support services to attract this emerging and important group, of which you are a part.

With the increase in the number of college students with learning disabilities, and the growth of services and programs to serve them, you can join the ranks of those who build one achievement upon another and succeed in their program of choice. There is never only *one* school or program that is just right for everyone, so plan on investigating every option in order to find the ones that seem the most likely to meet your particular needs.

The United States is able to boast of over 1,500 accredited four-year colleges. When two-year colleges and other non-accredited schools are counted, that number grows to over 3,400 choices to consider.

Your decision about continuing your schooling might have a critical impact on your life.

- The average college graduate earns 40 percent more over the course of their career than the average high school graduate—over $660,000 more than those without college degrees. Each year the gap grows wider and wider.

- Our economy is shifting to technology and high level service industries, where a college degree or advanced certification is generally required.

If you are a high school student with learning disabilities, interested in finding your place in college and in a career, read on. This book can help steer you through the maze of information you will encounter as you plan your future.

Why Choose College?

With over 3,000 colleges and university in the United States, it is clear that we are a country that values education. And educational professionals tell us that we do change as a result of a college experience. It may serve to:

- Help develop the **total person**
- Create **cultural awareness**
- Expand your **range of interests**
- Create more **humanitarian values** and attitudes
- Instill a greater **sense of tolerance**
- Develop **respect for the rights of others**
- Expose you to **community affairs** and **societal issues**

To get ready for a college program, you will need to prepare for the experiences you will most likely encounter. The more information that you have, the more confident you are likely to feel. Not having adequate information can easily add to your anxiety about the unknown and will make it harder for you to be on top of a new situation.

A Stepping-stone for Many

Several important factors account for the increased involvement in higher education of people with learning disabilities:

- Earlier and more accurate identification of students who have learning disabilities

- Improved delivery of special education services in elementary, middle, and high schools

- The understanding that any support provided for those with learning disabilities may enable them to unlock their potential in and beyond college

- A growing belief that a commitment to special education will enhance every aspect of our society

Once considered the privilege of an elite few, a college degree has now become a stepping-stone for all who pursue the American Dream. Back in 1950, about 40 percent of high school graduates went on to some form of higher education. But by 1992, two out of every three high school graduates were including higher education as part of their plan for life, in the hope of stepping up their career and economic future. Statistics show us that during the 40 or more years of most people's worklife, the difference in wages earned between a person with a college degree and someone with only a high school diploma will more than cover the costs of additional education. This is an investment that makes good sense to all those who can consider it, whether it is handled in the traditional way or in any other way that achieves the same goal.

Remember that *the value of higher education can never be measured in earnings alone*. The experience of learning and expanding your knowledge and intellectual growth—the self-discoveries, friendships, and personal contacts, along with residential life experiences—may color your development and have a lifelong impact on you. For a wealth of reasons, *it pays to go to college*!

Fortunately, for those with learning disabilities, the time has never been better. There are many college programs for you to consider. Your choice of college will depend on the type of education you decide you want and the kind of program that will best meet your needs.

The transition from high school to a college setting is difficult for most students and often more stressful for adolescents with learning disabilities. With research and careful planning, however, the college admissions process can be a time of discovery and accomplishment.

The important news is that there is a wide array of possibilities open to you. It's safe to say that there is a program available for every learning-disabled student who is determined to complete a two- or four-year program. You can always locate—or even transfer to—a school that will match your interests and your budget. A traditional four-year college may not be the right choice for everybody, but there are other options to consider, including a post–high school year (or *bridge*) program prior to entering college. This book can serve as your guide to a wide range of alternatives that you may wish to look into. It can provide you with the information you will need as you begin to investigate schools and their programs.

You will find many programs that may meet your particular needs. Colleges now have special offerings for students with learning disabilities. You will discover **special services** departments that serve the needs of all students with disabilities, including learning disabilities, as well as **learning skills centers** that focus solely on the needs of those students with learning problems.

You will need to be realistic and honest about yourself in *all* areas:

- Academic preparation
- Level of motivation
- Social skills
- Maturity
- Level of independence

Postsecondary Education

If you see yourself as a candidate for higher education, you need to familiarize yourself with the kinds of educational institutions that follow high school. Postsecondary education refers to any education or training you receive after you complete high school. It includes:

- All colleges and universities
- Vocational and technical schools
- Trade schools
- Business schools
- Adult education programs
- Continuing education programs

Community colleges

Many two-year institutions provide support services for students with learning disabilities. One important feature of a local community college is that you can live at home and commute to school if you still need to develop independent living skills. Be sure to refer to chapter 3, "A Closer Look at Community Colleges," for detailed information.

Small residential colleges

This is often a fine choice if you have a learning disability because of the ease with which you can interact with other students and with the faculty and staff. You must search carefully, however, as many smaller colleges do not have the budgets to offer comprehensive support programs.

Urban college or universities

Larger urban campuses are more likely to have the funds to support a wide array of special programs for students with learning disabilities. Nevertheless, this choice may mean large classes and a large student/faculty ratio, which can result in less interaction and less personal attention.

Vocational education programs

Finding a course of study that will prepare you for the labor market may be an excellent way to arm yourself with the necessary credentials to be part of the work force. The kind and quality of these programs vary widely, so it's best to contact the Director of Vocational Rehabilitation in your state for specific information about approved vocational education programs.

Depending upon your particular needs, you should be able to select a school or program with the expertise and resources to serve you best. Begin your search with the assistance of your high school guidance counselor or other faculty member who is aware of your special strengths and areas of weakness.

Share your hopes and dreams with your family, your friends, and your mentors. Listen to their points of view so that you can benefit from the insights of all those who care about your future. Keep in mind that the possibility for disappointment does exist. Even the high-achieving students without learning disabilities receive college rejection letters from schools, so you must be prepared for setbacks. But remember: your college education can inspire you to dream, shape your life, and give hope to your future. It may allow you to reach for the stars!

Are You Ready for College?

Many high school seniors view the idea of college with mixed emotions. Some students are relieved to have completed high school and may not care to have any additional classroom contact. Others may be somewhat interested in the idea of more education, but feel timid or discouraged about their chances for success in college. Yet many students may be determined to accept the challenge of completing a two- or four-year college program, and will make every effort to succeed.

Take the Challenge...And Succeed!

Choosing a college with great thought and care can put you on a successful track, with the support and back-up you will need to rely upon. If you are determined to give the college experience a try, you are fortunate. Never before has as much special assistance or awareness of the needs of the learning disabled been available.

If you are considering attending school away from home, you must be prepared to deal with a variety of areas and responsibilities in your college life, including:

- Budgeting your money
- Paying bills on time
- Doing chores, such as laundry and banking
- Shopping for clothes, supplies, and personal needs
- Managing your time
- Planning social activities
- Handling your medical needs
- Dealing with other adults—roommates, professors, college staff members
- Adjusting to new and unfamiliar situations
- Problem-solving when classroom and dorm issues arise

Separating from your family and living away from home require a great deal of independence in daily living skills. It is often easier for some students to pass an introductory literature course than to master living in a dormitory. While still in high school, it will be helpful for you to be aware of and develop important skills that you will need to use during your college years and thereafter. Such skills include:

- Self-advocacy
- Decision-making
- Problem-solving
- Knowing how to explain your specific disability to others
- Organizing and managing your time well
- Listening
- Following oral and written directions
- Staying "on task" without being distracted
- Knowing when to ask for help
- Finishing assignments on time
- Working independently
- Working in small groups
- Efficient notetaking

Criteria for Success

Motivation.   Motivation is critical. Most situations after high school demand hard work and commitment. Because you may require more time to grasp and complete assignments, and often must work more diligently, a high degree of motivation is essential. You must *really want to succeed.* Your motivation and determination may make the difference between success and failure in school.

Self-awareness.   Self-awareness of your own academic strengths and limitations is very important. It can mean the difference between self-advocacy and the use of support services, or unrealistic expectations and a sense of helplessness on the college campus.

Self-advocacy.   It's important that you learn how to discuss your limitations and explain to others what you need in order to work around these limitations. You are the one person best-equipped to know your own strengths and weaknesses. You will need to be able to state your specific needs in a clear and informed way, and to the appropriate people. This is referred to as self-advocacy.

While still in high school, there may be several people helping you as advocates. Counselors, teachers, your parents, or other professionals may be actively representing your best interests. In college you will have to take on some of that responsibility for yourself. Learning to become your own advocate (or *self-advocate*) is an important step in achieving your independence.

Study skills.   Good study skills are invaluable. Learning to organize your time to work independently, and knowing when to seek help when necessary and how to take advantage of all available resources, will better equip you to successfully complete your program.

Social and emotional factors.   Many factors will have a great impact on your success in school. Your ability to feel as though you really fit in and belong is critical. Often just one person—a fellow-student or even an interested staff or faculty member—can make a world of difference. You'll need someone to talk to, to air your concerns and fears with, and to share the ups and downs of this new situation.

Struggling with the Decision— Do You Have What It Takes?

You are not alone if you are concerned about whether or not you'll make it in college. Fear of failure is a common concern among high school students considering college, and certainly for most students with learning disabilities, who may have added pressures in a college setting.

- Do I have what it takes?
- Am I smart enough?
- Can I handle the workload?
- Will I be comfortable living away from home?

These questions and others plague many people when considering higher education. Oddly enough, *achievement really is unrelated to intelligence*. Your ability to achieve your goals in college will have everything to do with your **attitude**, **motivation**, and **self-discipline**. Success in college depends more on these factors than on actual levels of intelligence.

Don't forget to consider important differences that do exist between high school and the demands of a college-level program.

- College classroom time is generally 12 to 15 hours per week for a typical program, or even less if you decide to have a reduced course load. Your high school courses probably totaled between 25 and 30 hours per week.

- Because college-level learning is considered student-centered, you are expected to spend more time on independent reading and studying in preparation for each course. You will probably find that many college professors expect a higher level of academic proficiency than was accepted in high school.

- Another dramatic difference is your ability as a college student to make decisions. You will decide whether or not to go to class, whether or not to be prepared with assignments or homework projects, and whether you have studied for exams. No one is available to monitor this for you, so you will need to do a good job of planning your time and making the most of the school's resources.

Many college students, regardless of their backgrounds, have a weak sense of organization and time management and often neglect rules of promptness and planning. Is it possible that you need to make improvements in this area?

- Are you often disorganized?
- Do you have trouble starting projects…and then completing them on time?
- Do you plan and schedule time haphazardly?
- Do you do a poor job of managing your personal obligations?

Mastering some or all of these issues will keep you on the track of feeling capable and confident. Society tends to perceive you as a competent adult when you show that you are an independent self-manager.

Unfortunately, good organization and time management become very difficult for those with weak memories and a poor sense of order. You can rely on using **time tools** that are easily available, including:

- Watches, alarm clocks, and timers
- Calendars; daily, weekly, and long-range planners
- Organizers and checklists of things to do

Learn to set realistic goals and priorities for all of your assignments. Identify all the steps you will need to take to complete your tasks. Then gauge how much time you will need for each activity, so that you can plan your time realistically. You would not want to set aside only one hour for library research if you knew it would take you at least 30 minutes to get there and return, leaving you only half an hour to do your research. You will need to make every effort to minimize whatever serves as a distraction for you while you are working. Don't plan on studying in your dorm if your roommate will be blasting the stereo, or in a lounge if you know the chatting of others will disturb you. Identify an available study space that will work best for you.

Developing Skills for College

Take a look at the kinds of skills that college students are expected to have. Discover which areas need more of your attention, and work on strengthening them. Do you:

_____ Estimate how much time you need for projects and assignments?

_____ Allow enough time to complete what you need for the next day?

_____ Waste time or use it efficiently?

_____ Study in a space that is free of distractions?

_____ Always hand in assignments on time?

_____ Focus on your task, take breaks when you need them, and then return to the task?

_____ Ask for help when you need it?

_____ Take notes in class?

_____ Highlight key points in your notes so you can study from them?

_____ Use a tape recorder in class if you need to?

_____ Break large assignments into smaller parts and tackle one part at a time?

_____ Easily spot the central idea when you are reading?

_____ Review your class notes to reinforce your learning each day?

_____ Take notes on what you've read?

_____ Highlight key passages while reading?

_____ Make an outline for written assignments before you start to write?

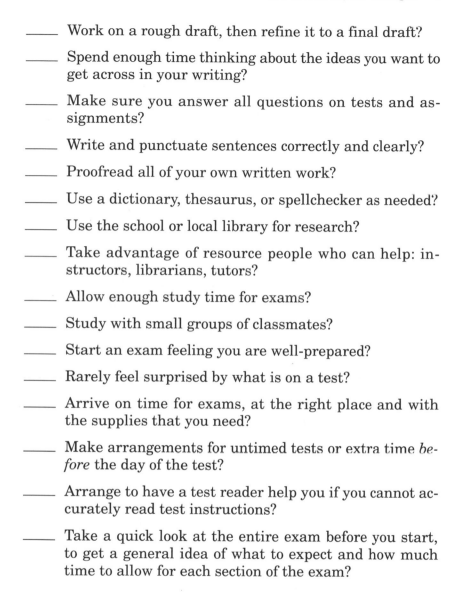

_____ Work on a rough draft, then refine it to a final draft?

_____ Spend enough time thinking about the ideas you want to get across in your writing?

_____ Make sure you answer all questions on tests and assignments?

_____ Write and punctuate sentences correctly and clearly?

_____ Proofread all of your own written work?

_____ Use a dictionary, thesaurus, or spellchecker as needed?

_____ Use the school or local library for research?

_____ Take advantage of resource people who can help: instructors, librarians, tutors?

_____ Allow enough study time for exams?

_____ Study with small groups of classmates?

_____ Start an exam feeling you are well-prepared?

_____ Rarely feel surprised by what is on a test?

_____ Arrive on time for exams, at the right place and with the supplies that you need?

_____ Make arrangements for untimed tests or extra time _before_ the day of the test?

_____ Arrange to have a test reader help you if you cannot accurately read test instructions?

_____ Take a quick look at the entire exam before you start, to get a general idea of what to expect and how much time to allow for each section of the exam?

How well did you fare on the checklist? College students with learning disabilities are often unprepared to meet the stresses and demands of college life and may have difficulty succeeding in this highly competitive environment. Educators are aware that these students not only need support services once they are in a postsecondary setting, but also need to be better prepared to face the challenges when moving from high school to college.

Easing the Transition from High School to College

A study of college students with learning disabilities showed that many students had concerns about their grades, followed by concerns about their study skills and their interpersonal difficulties. These students had a number of recommendations for high school students who are planning on attending college. These included:

- College exploration as early as the ninth grade
- Discussions about *work* as well as *school* options
- Career guidance
- Visiting colleges
- Having college students come to speak at high schools
- Getting help in money management and budgeting
- Learning social skills to make meeting new people easier
- Dealing with issues such as stress and managing time
- Developing a better understanding of their specific learning disability
- Improving study skills
- Learning how to be a self-advocate
- Learning how to use the library most effectively

Parents of high school students with learning disabilities have suggested the following when asked about their child's preparation for postsecondary options:

- High school students need to have a better sense of what they will encounter in college and need to know what they will be responsible for.
- They need to gather as much information as possible about their college choices in order to reduce their anxiety. Recommended are more opportunities to visit various campuses and the ability to meet college students, faculty, and special service professionals when they tour the campuses.
- Information about financial aid should be made more readily available, particularly details about *how* and *when* to apply.

Try to address as many of these issues as you can. It's an important investment that will pay off and make an important difference in your college experience.

Plan Your Senior Year Wisely

If you are a high school senior, the planning you do during your senior year is most important. Get a head start by keeping track of what needs to be done each month until graduation.

September

- Plan for visits to the colleges that you are considering.
- Meet with your guidance/college counselor to review your records and to ensure that you are registered for all the required courses you will need to graduate.
- Start to send out your completed college admissions applications.

October

- Concentrate on getting financial aid forms from your chosen colleges and work on gathering the information that you will need to submit those forms.
- Pay attention to **deadlines**.
- Make sure you go to all college fairs and financial aid sessions that your high school or school district sponsors.
- If you need to take ACT or SAT exams, make sure you register on time. If you want to re-take the tests to aim for better scores, start preparing for them *now*.

November

- Review the list of colleges that you've submitted applications to. Make sure that you have supplied all of the information and records that have been requested.

December

- Contact the residence halls of your chosen colleges to determine when you need to apply for dorm space. *Keep a record of these deadlines.*
- Get your financial aid needs analysis form from your guidance counselor and review what needs to be submitted.

January

- Gather together your parents' W-2 forms and other income-related papers that you will need for financial aid applications.
- Submit your completed financial aid needs analysis application.

March

- Answer all financial aid or admissions requests for additional information or documentation, so that your files are complete.

April

- Respond to college offers. Make your final decision and notify the school of your choice.
- Inform the schools you do not plan to attend of your decision.
- Once your financial aid award letter arrives, follow the directions you receive to get the process started.

May

- Be sure that all final high school transcripts are sent to the school you've decided to attend.

June/July

- Arrange to attend Freshman Orientation.
- Plan your budget for the school year.

- Shop for clothing, school gear, and accessories for your dorm room.
- If the college has supplied you with the name of your room-mate, contact him or her to introduce yourself and break the ice.

August

- Be sure you know what day and date you should be arriving on campus.
- Review your lists of all the items you want to take with you. Label or mark items of value, such as stereo equipment or cameras, with your name for security purposes.

Summary: A Checklist for Getting Ready for College

_____ Set realistic goals.

_____ Collect all of your high school special testing records before you graduate and make extra copies for your own files.

_____ Be sure that your psychological tests are current (within the last three years).

_____ Understand that Section 504 of the Rehabilitation Act of 1973 mandates schools to provide needed accommodations for you at your request.

_____ Be aware of all of your legal rights.

_____ Work on building up your study skills.

_____ Be realistic about your limitations and know what accommodations and strategies work best for you.

_____ Be equally aware of your stronger areas and be ready to describe them with comfort and ease.

_____ Practice independent living skills, such as managing your finances, doing your laundry, and learning basic cooking.

_____ Learn to be your own advocate.

_____ Make special arrangements for SAT or ACT exams if necessary.

_____ Closely examine and compare all college programs with special services for the learning-disabled.

_____ Arrange campus visits. Don't assume that everything you read in a college catalog is current or will be available to you.

_____ Be alert to all application deadlines.

_____ Thoughtfully select people to write letters of recommendation for you, if this is needed.

_____ Apply for financial aid for each school you apply to.

_____ When you hear your acceptance news:

- Notify all schools of your decision
- Pay the housing deposit when its due
- Plan your course schedule carefully so you don't overload

_____ Make sure you are motivated and determined to commit to the college of your choice.

2

What to Look for in a College

High school students with learning disabilities, whose educational needs have long been ignored, are now in a position to be actively recruited by colleges. State and federal legislation is now in place that will protect your rights. You and your parents need to take an active role in examining the kinds of programs offered, in order to find the one that will work best for you. The fact that you have a learning disability, and therefore have some special needs, means that you must consider all of the things that every other student needs to consider in choosing a college—plus a few more.

Considering Your Options

As record numbers of students with learning disabilities enroll in college, educators have had to examine their own attitudes, as well as their policies in the classroom and on the campus. By the mid-1980s, thoughtful educators were setting up on-campus learning centers. In some cases, this was just a resource for all students with disabilities, including those with physical handicaps. As the number of students with learning disabilities continued to rise, many campuses established learning centers staffed with special education professionals, who are trained to deal with the needs of the learning-disabled population, including:

- Counseling
- Tutoring
- Providing help in approaching faculty members to discuss accommodations in the classroom
- Counseling in self-advocacy strategies

Some colleges have very specific programs for students with learning disabilities. Others have a center that serves *all* students with special needs. Those schools with special services for the learning disabled are more likely to offer the expertise and resources for your particular requirements.

College life can be unpredictable, with many highs and lows. You will need to adjust to a new academic, as well as social, environment. Take heart; the resources and supports that are available *will* enable you to succeed. You will have a chance to be recognized for your potential and your achievement.

Remember to consider all your options, including community colleges. There you will find a wide array of occupationally oriented courses, in addition to liberal arts offerings. This can often be an important first step in the transition to a four-year institution, if you decide on obtaining a baccalaureate degree. Consider community college as a way of testing the waters of college life before taking the plunge into a four-year institution.

For some, the ideal college location is far enough away from home to provide an "away from home" feeling—yet close enough to allow for easy travel home on weekends or holidays. A two- to three-hour train or bus ride might be perfect for the student who relies on the support of friends or family at home.

Invest whatever time and energy is needed to determine the type of program that will serve *you* best. Ideal situations can include programs that ease the transition from high school and sharpen your basic skills at the same time:

- Academic programs that prepare you for the work force and promote intellectual growth
- Campus life that is diverse and offers an opportunity for personal growth

- Administrators with skills and resources to maintain or enhance the quality of the programs

Set your sights for what most college students want...*a program that offers the academic and social supports that will enhance your personal growth and prepare you for a career.* As you sort through possible choices, remember to keep in mind your particular requirements and the accommodations you need. The school you select must be prepared to offer you the kind of help and services you need, and you must match the supports you require to what the institution can provide. Before evaluating a college, it's best to begin by evaluating yourself, examining:

- Your abilities
- Your areas of weakness
- The kind of learning environment in which you work best
- The types of people you feel most at home with

Too many students apply to postsecondary schools for the wrong reasons, including where their buddies are going or the reviews the schools receive in college guides.

Before you decide on the level of support you need, you will have to ask yourself:

- How you learn best
- What aids and modifications you need

Merely choosing a school because it offers services for people with learning disabilities may not work well for you if the available services are not just what you require. If you are unsure about the specific accommodations you need, review your most recent educational evaluation with your school counselor or your tutors. They can give you feedback on your past performance. To form a total picture of what will be needed to make your college experience a success, keep in mind the pattern of your social shortcomings as well.

The selection of the best college program for you is a procedure that requires awareness of your needs as they relate to *all* of your strengths and weaknesses, and then researching schools and available programs to determine the resources that best mesh with your needs. There are many postsecondary institutions—large and small, public and private, urban and suburban—that offer a variety of important services. Traditional programs, as well as individually designed programs, should be considered to ensure that you reach for your goal in the college setting of your choice. Feel optimistic about functioning successfully in an educational system that has never been more supportive of nontraditional learners. And remember: Your own individual differences are your special assets. Each one of us has special needs as well as special abilities and talents.

What Do You Want from Your College Experience?

- An opportunity to prepare for your future?
- A chance to meet new people?
- An opportunity to be away from home and function independently?
- A comfortable environment for the next two to four years?
- A chance to challenge yourself at your own pace and to discover what you can accomplish?

Selecting the Right College

How much support you will want in college depends on your own personal needs.

Minimal Support Colleges

Consider attending a college that provides minimal support if your SAT scores are above 950 and if you needed minimum support services in high school. For example, you may have needed untimed tests or occasional tutoring. Colleges with minimal services generally do not take an active role in advocating for students with learning disabilities. You may find relatively little in the way of extra services, perhaps just enough for the school to meet federal regulations. Academic advisement or study centers are likely to be available to the entire student body and may not be adapted to your specific learning needs. However, for some students with learning disabilities, this level of support may be very workable. You would have to have a very clear sense of the specific accommodations and adaptations you need and make your own provisions for them to be put in place. For instance, you would need to know that you should take a light courseload or buy your textbooks in advance in order to be prepared for reading assignments. Good social skills and a sense of independence are especially important if you wish to attend a minimal support college.

Moderate Support Colleges

Consider these if your SAT scores range from 800–950. You will need to be a self-advocate for tutorials, counseling services, and your other needs. There may be a specially designated office or person on campus to assist you, as well as additional services. Your faculty liaison can intervene for you with other professors when such advocacy is needed. Frequently, your professors will modify course requirements to meet your needs. The focus of such a program is to help you adjust to the college situation, but you are expected to know when you need help and then ask for it.

Comprehensive Support Colleges

Support throughout your college years may be required, in which case you might consider a college which provides comprehensive services. These can be considered by students with a broad range of SAT scores and an average or above average IQ, and who have completed a college preparatory program. These colleges provide a wide array of academic counseling and services, including tutoring. Some programs focus on developmental skills, others on learning strategies. The support offered will vary widely from college to college. The focus of these intensive support programs is on adapting the program and services to your needs, rather than helping you adapt to the existing program. Schools that have the facilities and staffs for these programs welcome students with learning disabilities and are proud of their trained special education faculty.

What a comprehensive support program should provide

- A **Special Education Services Office** for students with learning disabilities, or other central coordinating area where you can go for assistance or information. This is where you would outline your specific accommodations or modification needs. Support groups and individual counseling might also be available from this facility. This center should act as a campus advocate for students with learning disabilities.

- A **staff of diagnosticians and trained professionals** who can administer and interpret psychoeducational evaluations for you.

- **Tutoring, writing clinics, and remedial services** in basic skills and in specific course content areas. Such offerings may be available on a one-to-one basis or in small study groups. Ask if individual assistance can be arranged and if fees are involved. Keep in mind that peer tutoring is usually the *least* effective way to gain compensatory skills. Small groups of ten or fewer led by a special education professional will be more effective if individual tutoring by a professional is not available. Chances are you may need help in:

  - Preparing outlines
  - Learning to take effective notes in class
  - Learning to use the campus library and other important resources
  - Making arrangements for untimed tests, oral exams, readers, scribes, etc.

- **Special education professionals** who are able to provide academic advice and help you avoid overloaded or unreasonable programs. In some cases, success is more attainable for students carrying a part-time load of 12 to 13 credits. Coursework can always be made up during summer or intersessions.

- **Learning disabilities specialists** may also serve as ombudsmen or advocates for you on the campus.

- **Special provisions** for reserved books, printed copies, taped texts, and other services, such as tape recorders, readers, note-takers, writers, or computer facilities.

- **Personal and career counselors** available to help you settle in and adapt to college life, and help you develop a career plan that recognizes your particular strengths and weaknesses.

- **Program planning** and/or priority registration.

- **Notification to instructors** about your needs, with your permission.

- **Special testing arrangements**.

- **Job placement services**.

- **Support groups and workshops** on learning strategies, self-advocacy, time management, independent living skills, budgeting, handling your finances, and so on.

Four-year institutions are more likely to have tougher entrance requirements than community colleges. Most colleges will require testing and will want to review your high school transcripts, or even your ranking within your high school class. Keep in mind that if you do decide to take the ACT or SAT test, you may request:

- A large print version of the test
- A separate distraction-free room
- Additional testing time
- A reader or the use of a tape recorder

Other Options

Bridge or College Prep Programs

These programs offer a post–high school year, and focus on developing academic skills and fostering social growth. Some of these programs can serve as an introduction to residential living and provide you with a structured academic and social environment away from home.

Independent Living Programs

These programs focus on fostering independent living skills, social skills, and vocational skills within the framework of a college setting. There is often an opportunity to work toward a certificate upon completion of the program, rather than a degree.

Residential Programs

This will allow the more mature student with learning disabilities the opportunity to live in an apartment or a residential complex and focus on developing basic living skills, such as career-planning and taking responsibility for personal needs.

If a traditional school setting is not right for you, you might consider a trade school or vocational education program. These schools can produce workers with fine career choices and earning potential.

Summary: Support Services— What's Out There

Minimal Support Colleges

- For SAT scores of 950 and above.
- Workable if you were successful with minimal intervention and support in high school.
- You need to be clear about your limitations and have the ability to ask for help when it is needed.

Moderate Support Colleges

- For SAT scores in the 800–950 range.

- You need to be a good self-advocate.
- The aim of the college is to *assist you in adjusting to the program*.

Comprehensive Support Colleges

- Open to a wide range of SAT scores.
- Offerings may include skills remediation, access to learning disabilities specialists, specialized courses, tutors, counseling services, and so on.
- The aim of the college is to *adapt the program to your needs*.

Transitional Programs (Bridge or College Prep)

- A post–high school year focusing on academic and study skills development, and social growth.

Independent Living Programs

- Fosters independent living skills, social and vocational skills.

Residential Programs

- Focuses on developing basic living skills and taking responsibility for personal needs.

Choosing a College That's Right for You

Carefully review the services and facilities each college claims to offer and select those that seem most promising. Keep in mind the size, expense, and location of the school. Balance this against your own educational interests and the services that you know you will require.

- Consider small to mid-sized campuses with student/faculty ratios of about 12 to 1, or less. These will provide a more personal atmosphere.

- Although larger colleges can often offer more elaborate services, they can also feel impersonal and lack the responsive environment that most freshmen need.

- Aim to match your particular needs to the kinds of services and supports provided. Don't bank on the recommendations of friends and neighbors. Your requirements will probably not be the same as theirs.

- Consider schools that allow you to change your major. When colleges are eager to assist you in finding the program that best suits you, you may save additional time by not having to make up extra coursework in a newly chosen area of study.

- Look for services that will offer you instruction in: oral speaking, listening, remedial reading, spelling, note taking, studying, outlining and summarizing, planning and writing papers, research techniques, test-taking strategies, time management, memory/concentration techniques, computer skills, and word processing.

- Look for these counseling-related services: academic advisement, personal counseling, career and life planning.

- Look for programs that will offer these kinds of accommodations: priority registration, untimed or extended-time tests, distraction-free rooms for exams, oral testing, textbooks on tape, personal readers and test readers, tutors, proofreading services, use of tape recorders in class lectures, machines that transpose print to speech and speech to print.

Visiting the Campus

Deciding on the program and college that is best for you will be a difficult task for you and your parents. Colleges differ in their mission and the focus of their programs. *Ask as much as you feel you need to know to determine an institution's philosophy and how it is implemented.* Remember that the glossy brochures and attractive videotapes are advertisements. They are the college's way of promoting itself and attracting students. The most important thing that you can do is to visit the schools you are seriously considering. After the school tour, walk around the campus and:

- Talk to the students about their likes and dislikes.

- See if you can arrange to sit in on a class or two.

- Have a snack or a meal in the cafeteria.

- Review the campus bulletin boards to get a sense of campus life and discover what is happening on the weekends.

- Ask questions not mentioned in the brochure or student handbook, such as the number of dropouts or transfers out of the school each year, or the job placement statistics for the recent past.

- Ask about student activities and social and cultural events.

- Visit the dorms and off-campus housing to get the true flavor of what life on *that* campus is really like. If possible, spend a night in the dorm.

- Make contact with the office or center for Special Services. View the physical space critically. It should be calm, well-organized, and welcoming. Talk to staff members to get a sense of how involved with their students they seem to be. A well-trained and caring professional staff can help make the difference between failure and success during this important period in your life.

- Try to contact graduates of the college, if at all possible. This will give you a chance to get their points of view, both positive and negative.

Visiting the Learning Center

Be sure to plan your visit to include time spent in the Learning Center. Arrange in advance of your trip to meet with the director and, if possible, some of the other staff members. Plan on visiting when students are being served, so that you can assess the level of friendliness, care, and concern the students receive. Spend time observing how busy and involved the students seem and determine if the environment feels comfortable and welcoming. Don't be fooled by a deluxe setting or fancy exterior. Important work can be handled in the most modest surroundings. Try to talk with students who are using the facility. They can give you the best sense of how helpful and responsive the center *really* is. Recent graduates of the program are also a wonderful source of

information. The director may be happy to share names of satisfied graduates with you. If you are able to contact them or their
parents, do so.

Be aware of the professional staff's training and experience.
Those with a background in special education or learning disabilities often can provide more comprehensive services. Don't
be timid. It is reasonable to explore the background and credentials of the tutors and the counselors. Certainly the director or
head of the Learning Disabilities program should be a trained
professional.

Be sure to ask if the range of services offered will cost you additional money, or if they are included in the price of tuition. You
should also ask if the college requires a psycho-educational evaluation. Some schools will ask you for an independent evaluation
prior to admissions; others may want to do their own testing. If
that is the case, ask about test fees. Some schools will not offer
the testing, nor require it as part of their admissions process.
Generally speaking, schools that require your psycho-educational profile use it to determine your needs, and tend to be interested in maximizing your experience on their campus.

The program you select should focus on refining and enhancing
your knowledge, skills and strategies for dealing with your disabilities. You will have a chance to emerge as a more independent
learner and a more independent worker, armed with knowledge
about how you can be most successful.

Trust your own feelings. If you visit a campus and feel uncomfortable, it's probably not the best match for you. Your gut reactions are important.

Summary: A Checklist for Evaluating College Programs

After your campus visits, try to answer these questions to determine which program offers you what you need:

_____ Is there an office with learning disabilities or special education professionals who will be helpful in planning
your program as to a reasonable course load and sequential and well-balanced courses. Do they place an

emphasis on placing you in courses that reflect your strengths or interests in the first semester?

_____ Is basic skill remediation handled on a one-on-one basis by special education professionals?

_____ Are modified exam procedures—such as untimed, oral, typed, taped or dictated tests—possible?

_____ Are books and printed handouts available on tape?

_____ Can you tape classroom lectures?

_____ Are readers and note takers available?

_____ Are communications between the learning disabilities staff and the regular faculty open, frequent, and welcomed?

_____ Is the faculty supportive and willing to learn about the learning disabled students?

_____ Does the administration support the learning disabilities program?

_____ Are faculty and administration aware of the requirements of Section 504 of the Rehabilitation Act of 1973 with regard to reasonable accommodations and program requirements for the handicapped?

_____ Are personal counseling, support groups, and faculty advocates available?

_____ Are diagnosticians or clinicians available to do evaluations if you need them?

_____ Are career and life planning courses and counselors available to help you in your choice of major and to determine realistic career goals?

_____ What is the availability of group or individual career planning services that might include workshops, mentors, internships, work-study programs, and job referrals?

_____ Are learning centers and writing, math, or reading labs available on campus with specialists who understand the unique needs of the learning disabled?

_____ Are basic computer courses and computer facilities there for you?

_____ If needed, can you get help in these areas: oral presentation, listening skills, remedial reading, remedial math, spelling, note taking, outlining, summarizing, studying, highlighting, test-taking strategies, planning and writing papers, library and research skills, memory and concentration techniques?

In addition to services that relate specifically to your special educational needs, you will want to ensure that the college of your choice offers extracurricular activities, promotes faculty participation, and has a strong health services department. You will also broaden your horizons outside the classroom through field experience programs, internships, and other activities that can make your education really come to life!

Summary: How to Find *Your* Best College

- Gather information about schools that have programs of interest to you.

- Consider the accommodations you will need and the level of services you want.

- Carefully investigate the availability of accommodations and special services in the programs or schools you select.

- Have a current psycho-educational evaluation available. Under the Individuals with Disabilities Education Act, you can get a free evaluation in your high school. Be sure that it provides a specific diagnosis for the college admissions professionals you will be dealing with.

- Understand the nature of your particular learning disability. Work to become comfortable talking about it to others and be familiar with what accommodations you will need in the classroom.

- Learn to be a self-advocate. Always sit in on any high school planning meetings with your parents and school officials. Participate in all decisions and give your input on what works best for you. By the time you get to college, you'll be ready to do this by yourself with ease.

3

A Closer Look at Community Colleges

More than half of all freshmen entering public and private colleges in the country are students who have chosen to enroll in **community colleges**. This impressive trend forges on as community colleges continue to become a critically important part of postsecondary education.

Students are wisely making more use of community colleges to prepare themselves for a career—or to prepare themselves to transfer to a four-year institution at a later date. When you consider the modest tuition and the quality of educational programs available in our nation's community colleges, it's easy to understand why.

Also called **junior colleges** or **two-year colleges**, community colleges can be public or private institutions. Programs can prepare you for professional technical careers, as well as for transferring to a four-year or *senior* college to obtain a **bachelor's** (or **baccalaureate**) **degree**.

Community colleges often offer some significant advantages:

- Lower tuition than many four-year institutions
- The ability to live at home and commute to school
- A chance to test if you are really ready for college
- The availability of highly specialized occupational programs

- Smaller student body than at many four-year colleges, which may allow for a closer student/faculty relationship
- Strong industry affiliations
- No SAT entrance requirement

A two-year program in a community college may provide you with the background for job security, financial reward, and future growth.

With impressive facilities and reasonable rates, no wonder community colleges have captured our attention. Their growing reputation has convinced many high school students to consider them as an option, or as a part of a long-range plan that might eventually include a four-year college to obtain a bachelor's degree.

Upon graduating from high school, some students have still not firmed up their career goals. Others do not have the ability to finance the often exorbitant tuition fees. As the cost of higher education rises in both private and public colleges, the idea of attending a community college for two years is very appealing and practical.

For students who are not able to meet the entrance requirements of four-year colleges, the community college system is a welcome alternative. Many of these schools have liberal admissions policies. In most cases you will have to prove that you are a high school graduate or have an Equivalency Diploma (also referred to as a GED). You can always test the waters, without making a major financial commitment, by registering for one or two courses that appeal to you. For students whose high school records are weak, the community college system can provide you with another chance to move up the educational ladder.

Community colleges also have an excellent reputation for offering special services for students with learning disabilities, as part of the more affordable tuition picture. If you prefer to think about a college experience away from home, perhaps a community college in a location not too far from your friends and family will provide you with that opportunity.

Advantages of Attending a Community College

Think about community colleges for a variety of reasons:

- The financial advantage
- A trial run
- Forging ahead educationally
- Industry contacts
- Transfer options

Financial Advantage

The tuition at a community college may be one of the best educational values available. If you are able to attend an in-state community college and live at home while studying, you will be saving even more money. If a four-year degree interests you consider spending your first two years at a community college. That way, you will save on tuition to apply towards a third and fourth year elsewhere. This does mean that you *must* be ready to transfer to another institution midway through your college career, which can be disruptive. But many students who begin their college careers in community colleges make the switch successfully. Moreover, many community colleges have started to forge links with nearby four-year colleges and universities to help make the transfer of credits an easy process. Some states, such as Illinois and Florida, actually hold a certain number of spaces in third-year classes expressly for community college transfers.

A Trial Run

If you are not quite sure that college is the right choice for you, a community college is the ideal place for you to test the water. You can matriculate and carry a full-time load (generally 13–16 credits) or a smaller, part-time credit load. Or you can experiment by just signing up for one or two courses of interest to you as a **Continuing Education** or **Adult Education** student.

Some community colleges will even grant credit to you for demonstrating expertise in a particular skill area. This could allow you to move on to a more advanced level or excuse you from taking a specific course. For example, if you are fluent in a foreign language or have outstanding computer knowledge or other expertise, it may make sense to look into **Advanced Placement** or **Prior Learning Assessment** (referred to as PLA) at your community college.

Forging Ahead

Many students are clear about *not* wanting to continue beyond a two-year associate-level college degree. You may feel eager to enter the labor market with some basic skills under your belt, and may do as well with two solid years of work experience combined with a community college degree as you would with the two years spent working towards a bachelor's degree. In some high-tech fields, such as the computer industry, workers with a community college degree may in fact be further along their career path and earning more salary after two years spent in industry than those who spend time completing a four-year Computer Science degree. On-the-job training and learning, as well as a stable work history, are important credentials to bring to an employer. Some workers will still find that having the baccalaureate degree is needed for future career moves, so remember that you *can* return to complete a four-year degree at any time.

Industry Connections

Many community colleges offer specialized vocational programs and can provide wonderful partnerships with local employers. These industry members rely heavily on graduates of those programs for their hiring needs. Look into the **Internship** and **Work-Study** (sometimes called **co-op** or **cooperative education**) **programs** that are offered in a wide variety of occupational areas.

Community colleges are an important feature of our higher education system. Don't think of a two-year college as an extension of high school or as simply a mini-version of a senior college. They have their own special identity and make a significant contribution to higher education.

Community colleges have truly been "discovered" as a great buy for quality education. They are now fully accepted in the educational mainstream.

"The community college, with close ties to the community and industries it serves, is the institution in our society best equipped to help Americans prepare to live and work in the coming century."

President Allan Hershfield
Fashion Institute of Technology
New York City

Transfer Options

Many students who choose to attend a community college are planning to eventually move on to a four-year institution. Their goal is to obtain a bachelor's degree. By now, all segments of our educational system acknowledge the validity of the two-year degree and the path it leads to for so many.

Generous transfer-credit policies are being established nationwide as more and more four-year colleges are welcoming students who have proven their ability to complete a two-year degree. Whenever possible, plan in advance, so you are sure that the courses you take in a community college are transferable to the four-year school of your choice. Most four-year colleges accept transfer students, some more enthusiastically than others. At some schools, transfer students are given priority for junior- and senior-level course openings. Other schools accept only a few transfer students and give their attention to those students who entered as freshmen. Still, it's interesting to note that some senior colleges report that community college transfer students actually do better than those who come on board as freshmen!

Four-year colleges and universities will only accept transfer credits from schools that are formally recognized by regional, national, or professional educational agencies. It is very important that the two-year college you select to attend is **accredited**. This means that the programs meet minimum levels of acceptable educational quality. School administrators and admissions professionals should be willing to discuss their institution's accreditation status with you, and it is usually mentioned in catalogs and other printed materials that schools provide to prospective students.

As you research four-year schools, you will discover that admissions requirements vary. This may depend on the popularity of the school and the demand for a particular program. You will probably need to show proof of completed coursework or your transcript, satisfactory test scores, and an academic record that meets a certain standard.

It is even possible to transfer from several community colleges if your educational path takes that direction. Schools usually will accept those courses that they decide are transferable to their programs, regardless of how many accredited schools are involved.

Be prepared, however, to have one four-year school accept a course that another school will not. Entrance requirements for each institution must reflect that school's mission. Course acceptability will be judged differently by different colleges. Whatever you submit for a college to consider for transfer credit must be evaluated at the *same* level as a similar course offered by that institution.

Keep in mind that transferring from a community college has become an accessible option for higher education. It is a practical and economical choice for millions of students.

4

A Variety of Learning Styles

"How you learn is just as important as what you learn." You probably have known this since your early days in school. Educational professionals now know it as well, and there is research to validate the fact that *people learn in very different ways*. Some of us need to see and touch, others need to hear information, and yet others prefer to write down new material in order to learn it. There is no one single way to learn—and certainly no one *right* way to learn. Learning occurs in many ways.

And not every learning problem is the same. We all vary in the way in which we process information best. We now know that success in learning is not only a feature of our intelligence, but a combination of a multitude of other factors.

Determining Your Own Learning Style

You may be able to determine the best approach to your own style of learning by identifying:

- If visual, auditory, or tactile information is easiest for you to deal with
- If individual or small group instruction makes the most sense for you

Understanding your own particular learning style may make it easier for you to determine what accommodations you will need in college, and will enable you to ask for specific kinds of assistance from your school's Learning Skills Center or Learning Disabilities Office.

In attempting to learn new things, all of us—including people who do not have a learning disability—find we have our own style. Some have an easier time **reading** instructions or information, while others will find it easier to understand what is **spoken** or **read** to them. You may already be aware of the type of learning that feels best for you. If you are not quite sure of what suits you best, go through the following short exercises, which will help you identify your learning preferences.

Check the response that best fits your own experiences. Decide how you would react most frequently in each situation.

You generally remember more from a class lecture when:

_____ 1. You don't take notes but try to listen carefully

_____ 2. You sit close to the lecturer and pay attention to him or her

_____ 3. You take notes even though you may not bother to re-read them

You can solve problems best by:

_____ 1. Talking issues over with friends

_____ 2. Organizing yourself with lists, charts, schedules, and the like

_____ 3. Pacing the floor or some other kind of physical activity

You can remember telephone or fax numbers best by:

_____ 1. Repeating them out loud

_____ 2. Visualizing the number in your mind

_____ 3. Writing the number down

It's easiest to learn new material by:

_____ 1. Listening to someone explain it to you

_____ 2. Watching someone show you how to do something

_____ 3. Trying to do it by yourself

The things you remember most clearly from a movie or television show are:

_____ 1. The music and the dialogue

_____ 2. The costumes and the scenery

_____ 3. The feelings you had while watching

When you try to remember something, you:

_____ 1. Try to visualize it in your mind

_____ 2. Try to recreate in your mind the conversations or sounds that occurred

_____ 3. Try to recall your feelings at the time

It would be easiest for you to learn a foreign language by:

_____ 1. Listening to instructional tapes

_____ 2. Using books

_____ 3. Taking a language class in which you read and write

If you are not certain about how a word should be spelled, you:

_____ 1. Sound it out

_____ 2. Try to visualize the way the word looks

_____ 3. Write it down in several ways and pick the spelling that looks right

The kind of reading you like best is:

_____ 1. Dialogue between characters

_____ 2. Creative and descriptive paragraphs

_____ 3. Action stories

It's easiest to remember new people you meet by:

_____ 1. Their names, as you often forget their faces

_____ 2. Their faces, as you often forget names

_____ 3. Their particular features or unusual mannerisms

You can easily be distracted by:

_____ 1. Noises

_____ 2. People

_____ 3. Surroundings

Which of these choices appeals most to you?

_____ 1. Talking with a friend

_____ 2. Watching TV

_____ 3. Relaxing on a comfortable couch

Add the number of your checkmarks to responses numbered 1, 2, and 3 and indicate the results here:

#1 checkmarks = _____	Auditory	You learn best by hearing.
#2 checkmarks = _____	Visual	You learn best by seeing.
#3 checkmarks = _____	Tactile or Kinesthetic	You learn best by doing or touching.

Note where your highest tally is. Does this seem right for you?

Here's another chance to learn more about your learning style. Check all the statements that you feel are fairly accurate for you. Work with someone who knows you well if you are not sure of how to respond. Some statements will not describe you perfectly, but check the one that comes closest.

I.

_____ You have a tough time copying written information, and you tend to leave things out when you copy material.

_____ You have better luck spelling a word correctly by sounding it out, rather than by writing it.

_____ Your handwriting is generally hard to read and sloppy.

_____ You have an easier time recalling something if you repeat it or say it aloud.

_____ You make small errors, like writing on the wrong line or using the wrong math sign.

_____ You are not too observant. Minor details, such as new clothing someone is wearing, might not get your attention.

_____ You occasionally reverse letters or numbers. You might even leave out some words when you are writing.

_____ You would rather have someone read to you than read material yourself.

_____ You have an easier time remembering something that was told to you than remembering something that you read.

_____ You would rather give an oral report than write one.

II.

_____ You prefer to show someone how to do something rather than tell them how to do it.

_____ You need to write things down, or make a mental picture for yourself, in order to remember them.

_____ You sometimes need to have things repeated because you weren't listening carefully.

_____ You often cannot think of a familiar word when you're talking, even when you know exactly what you'd like to say.

_____ You find it easier to figure out how to do something, rather than have someone explain it to you.

_____ You may forget what you hear, such as a telephone message, unless you write it down.

_____ You would often prefer to simply answer "yes" or "no" to a question rather than give a detailed answer.

_____ You sometimes use the wrong word when you're talking.

_____ You can do many things that would be hard for you to explain to others, like building or repairing something.

_____ You need to silently say the alphabet to yourself in order to remember the proper sequence of letters.

III.

_____ You do not become easily lost, even when in unfamiliar surroundings.

_____ You avoid reading directions. You'd rather just start doing the task.

_____ It's hard for you to sit at a desk and study for any length of time.

_____ You learn best when someone shows you how to do something and you can then try it on your own.

_____ You think and study better when you can move around.

_____ You solve problems through trial and error, rather than with an organized step-by-step approach.

_____ When you can't recall a familiar word, you'll say "you know" or "what do you call it."

_____ It would be hard for you to give clear verbal instructions or directions.

_____ You need to take breaks often when you are studying or preparing for an exam.

_____ You'd rather see someone else do something first, before you attempt to do it.

Now tally the checkmarks you entered on each list.

Auditory Learners

If you checked the most items on list I, you are probably more of an **auditory learner**. You learn and remember best by hearing and then repeating words silently to yourself. Hearing and speaking are critical to your learning. *Sounds, rather than what you see, are easier for you to remember*.

Tips for Auditory Learners

- Listen carefully to all information discussed in class.
- Sit close to the lecturer to avoid distraction by others.
- Try to keep your eyes focused on the lecturer.
- If you find that you distract yourself with books, pens, and so on, clear your desk and study area. Only deal with the text or the notebook that you need at that time.
- Repeat important instructions or information to yourself silently, or aloud, when you are not using a tape recorder.
- Make up jingles that rhyme or cute phrases to help you remember important items.
- Read your work and say the problems you're working on out loud. Do the same for the answers.
- Get as many tapes of textbooks as you can.
- Tape your class lectures and your study sessions.
- Learn to rely on your auditory memory as much as possible.

Visual Learners

Visual learners probably checked more items on list II. *Looking, seeing, and visualizing information are more important for you than hearing that same information*.

Tips for Visual Learners

- Your eyes are your pathway to help you learn.
- Pay close attention to charts, notes on the blackboard, printed handouts, and other written information.
- Take notes in all of your classes.

- Try to rewrite your notes if you have the time.
- Write down your homework assignments and due dates.
- Write lists of all things you need to do, to study, and to complete.
- Always keep a memo pad and a pocket calendar with you.
- Try to use flashcards or 3" × 5" index cards to identify the information you need to know for exams.
- Try to form a picture in your mind of a tough word you are trying to spell, rather than sounding it out.

Tactile Learners

If most of your checks were on list III, you tend to be a **tactile** or a **kinesthetic learner**. You tend to understand your work best when you are actively and physically involved in the learning of it. *You have the ability to learn by a "hands-on" method of experiencing or performing the activity to be learned.*

Tips for Tactile Learners

- Take advantage of lab or studio courses, as opposed to straight lecture classes, if you have a choice.
- You profit most from handling materials. Consider building models or giving demonstrations to the class, as opposed to handing in more traditional written reports or term projects.
- You enjoy reading material that is action-filled.
- You will most likely study best in a small study group or working with a study partner.
- You are not impulsive or impatient; you merely have the need to move on to other activities after a while.
- When writing, jot down words whose spelling you're unsure of, to see if it "looks" correct.
- When you study, change locations each time you take a break, to help stretch your legs and give you a chance to move about.

Individual and Collaborative Study Situations

Here's a simple exercise to help you determine if you work and learn best by yourself or with others. It is useful to understand whether you work best on an individual or collaborative setting.

IV.

_____ I get more work done when I work alone.

_____ I prefer not to ask classmates for help.

_____ I like to try to solve a problem by myself, rather than work with a small group of students.

_____ I can work much faster and much more thoroughly when I work alone.

_____ It's hard for me to concentrate if I am interrupted or distracted by others.

V.

_____ I feel I can accomplish more when I work with other students.

_____ I often gain more from a classroom discussion than I do from reading the text.

_____ I think better when I work with someone else.

_____ I like to help other students with school projects.

_____ I can learn as much from other classmates as I can from the teacher.

Three or more checks on list IV may suggest that you truly prefer to study and learn by yourself. You want to learn at your own pace and in your own style, without being distracted, interrupted, or sidetracked by others.

Three or more checks on list V may indicate your preference for a collaborative approach to learning. Study groups, teams, or even just another student as a study partner will be helpful to you.

Understanding Your Personal Preferences

Take note of the various ways you learn. Is one clearly preferred by you or do you feel you learn best by using strategies from more than one category? Think about whether the results of the informal exercises are what you thought they might be. Is this how you would have described yourself, or is this new information you have learned about yourself?

This may be information you will want to discuss with a college instructor or a counselor as you think about the services you will need in college. View your particular learning preference as a strength that you now understand. Then build it up and rely on it to work for you.

Most of us have more than one way in which we integrate and learn information, but frequently have a preference for a particular learning style. Don't worry if you cannot identify a clear-cut preference. Just try to familiarize yourself with your own style of learning, and start to use the tips that make sense for you.

Summary: Learning Styles

Visual Learners

Visual learners generally:

- Have difficulty with spoken directions
- Find it hard to follow lectures and discussions
- Usually need to see something in order to learn it
- Learn best by seeing and watching demonstrations
- Prefer to write things down
- Have a vivid imagination, often think in terms of pictures
- Like to be prepared with notes, charts, graphs, and the like

Visual learners should try to:

- Use graphics to aid in learning, such as illustrations, maps, slides, videos

- Color code their notes and files from different courses
- Write down as much as they can

Auditory Learners

Auditory learners generally:

- Need to hear it to learn it
- Can't follow written directions easily
- Don't pick up cues from the body language or facial expressions of others
- Learn best by verbal instructions from others
- Are easily distracted by sounds
- Remember best by repeating things out loud or to themselves
- Often will remember names and forget faces
- Like classroom discussions and hearing other students' thoughts and opinions

Auditory learners should try to:

- Make use of taped textbooks and lectures
- Listen to those tapes frequently
- Participate in class discussions
- Request a reader for exams

Tactile Learners

Tactile learners generally:

- Learn best through a hands-on approach
- Enjoy physical activity as part of the learning process
- Have difficulty sitting still and attending to the task in class
- Learn best by being directly involved
- Like to stand close to the people they are talking or listening to

- Love to draw and doodle rather than pay close attention in class

Tactile learners should try to:

- Master physical skills, such as sports, dance, gymnastics, and mechanics
- Study in short blocks of time rather than extended periods
- Take frequent breaks when studying
- Have as many experiential learning opportunities as possible, such as lab and studio courses or field work

5

Understanding Your Learning Disability

You may already know what it's like to be distracted and unfocused because you are bombarded by the sights and sounds around you, or to want to communicate something but be unable to do it properly. You know what it feels like to try to read a book or do a math problem and get confused by the numbers and the letters in front of you. These and a great range of other difficulties are part of the daily frustration that is experienced by people with learning disabilities.

A learning disability is often called the *hidden* or *invisible* handicap. Unlike some who walks with a cane or uses a hearing aid, a person with a learning disability gives no visible signs that he or she has a particular problem. Most people simply *do not realize* that your difficulty in processing information causes you to cope with many daily situations in a very different way than others. It is often hard for others to realize the frustration and pressures you deal with as you cope with learning, as well as with daily life.

The Difficulties of Learning Disabilities

There is no easy way to define the learning-disabled student, nor is there a typical profile. Each young adult with a learning disability has a wide range of strengths and weaknesses, just like young adults who are more traditional learners. However, the processes that generally work well for most others in gathering, processing, storing, and retrieving information do not work smoothly for the learning disabled. It is a dysfunction in the areas of:

- Reading
- Spelling
- Writing
- Math
- Comprehension
- Memory
- Attention

What this means is that you have had to work harder and longer to keep up with the accelerating levels of school work each year.

Your academic performance and behavior may be a real puzzle to others. For example:

- You may think logically and clearly, but be unable to write your thoughts in a simple paragraph.
- You may be alert and knowledgeable, but have difficulty following directions.
- Perhaps your handwriting or your coordination is awkward.
- Processing information or solving problems may be confusing for you.
- Sometimes muscles are affected, making it a chore just to hold a pen or pencil and complete written assignments or play certain sports.

You may have had little success in your past school experiences, or feel as if you have failed in making and keeping friends. With all this to deal with your self-esteem might be dangerously low!

What's more, it's unusual to have just one isolated symptom. Most people with learning disabilities have a combination of disorders. You may have a group of conditions that affect your ability to learn and cause you to achieve below your potential. Take heart: You do have the potential to perform better!

Adolescents with learning disorders often develop notions about their learning problems. Those misconceptions may be worse than the disorder itself. Too often they believe that they are hopelessly defective, even that they are "losers," since any "normal" person would not have *their* problems on a daily basis.

As a young adult with a learning disability, you need to recognize that you are neither defective nor perfectly typical. *You learn differently*...but you do learn!

Handling the Stress of a Learning Disability

Everyone has imperfections. We all need to learn to work around them, compensate for them, and wisely develop other skills that we can use with ease. However, for many with learning disabilities, the stress of hiding their disability from others saps much needed energy. Feelings of frustration, inadequacy, and anger are fairly common. There are often other problems among the learning disabled caused by sheer frustration, as when relatively simple tasks become incredibly difficult to start and to complete. It may also be hard to make and keep friends, which is a critical skill for every adolescent. This problem often surfaces due to the inability to properly read the social cues of others or appropriately interpret their responses. However, with appropriate services you can become a more independent learner, armed with knowledge of how to succeed and how to survive.

Education professionals are clear on one important fact. **People with learning disabilities are not retarded or dull or dumb**. A learning disability *never* refers to an inability to learn, or to a less than normal intelligence.

Many people find clever ways to cope with and overcome or complement certain aspects of their disability. In fact, a great many people cope with learning issues and learning problems. Experts now estimate that it is likely that as much as 10 percent of the population may struggle with learning disabilities. That is well over 25 million Americans!

Men tend to be three to four times more likely than women to have learning problems. And it is very common for a learning disability to be passed on in families, leading experts to believe that there is a real genetic link.

You may have experienced several of these common symptoms of a learning disability.

In childhood

- Difficulty expressing yourself
- Difficulty learning tasks, such as telling time or tying your shoelaces
- Mixing up the order of letters and numbers
- Difficulty learning to read
- Difficulty learning the words of songs or rhymes
- Distractibility or inattentiveness
- Difficulty following directions
- Confusion between left and right

In adolescence

- Inability to sequence numbers or events
- Slow reading with poor comprehension
- Poor spelling
- Difficulty organizing ideas
- Difficulty finding the appropriate words
- Difficulty remembering the names of people and places
- Low self-esteem as a result of past frustrations

There Is No Relation between Learning Disabilities and Intelligence

The label "learning disability" was actually coined in 1963 by Dr. Samuel Kirk, who wanted to acknowledge those students who were experiencing academic distress but seemed typical in other areas of their lives. In the more recent past there have been a variety of labels for learning disabilities—minimal brain damage, minimum cerebral dysfunction, dyslexia, and so on. A person with a learning disability is *not* a slow learner. In fact, you may often function at high levels, but find certain specific areas of learning more difficult to handle.

As with people without learning disabilities, learning-disabled students range from low to average to superior intellectual abilities. Some may even fall into the gifted category. Students are diagnosed as learning disabled when test scores show **a major gap between intellectual potential and actual achievement**. Federal regulations for identifying learning disabilities include a significant difference in capability and achievement in one of these areas:

- Listening comprehension

- Oral expression

- Written expression

- Basic reading skill and comprehension

- Math computation and reasoning

People with learning disabilities are often called "lazy and unmotivated" because of their inability to perform consistently. This inconsistency is a major symptom of a student with a learning disability and is *truly unrelated* to effort and to motivation. Special education professionals are needed to intervene and to help break the cycle of chronic failure. You need to begin to fully accept that a learning disability is *not* the result of:

- Mental retardation

- Emotional disturbances

- Visual, hearing, or motor handicaps

- Cultural or economic disadvantages

- Lack of motivation

- Poor academic background

Coping with a Learning Disability

Unfortunately, a learning disability is not a condition that will go away or that you will outgrow as you mature. Indeed, not so long ago it was thought that the invisible handicap of the learning disabled was a problem that children would outgrow.

There are many types and combinations of symptoms that vary from mild to severe. Some people with learning disabilities compensate so well that their problems are barely detectable. Others need extra help to learn how to compensate for a range of disabilities. Those with learning disabilities may have exceptional talents, but they cannot begin to uncover them and share them with the world until they learn the strategies that will allow them to do so. Your learning disability is a life-long situation that you need to learn to cope with, as it will impact your school experience, your social life, your work performance, and many other aspects of your daily life.

The most commonly described characteristics of learning-disabled students include difficulty with:

- Written expression
- Spoken language
- Reading and comprehension
- Spelling
- Problem-solving
- Work and study habits

Learning-disabled students themselves frequently also report difficulties in:

- Math problems
- Short attention span
- Disorganization
- Comprehension
- Time and space confusion
- Impulsivity
- Social problems

- Distractibility
- Restlessness
- Memory problems
- Low stress tolerance

Translated into real life for the prospective college student, it can easily mean you will have to expect problems with:

- Note taking
- Math computation
- Memorizing
- Problem-solving
- Reading assignments
- Managing tasks
- Outlining important material
- Organizing your time
- Setting priorities
- Researching and preparing for exams

Successful learning-disabled students have learned to:

- Develop coping and survival strategies
- Use appropriate accommodations
- Develop good organizational skills
- Understand their disability as well as their abilities
- Advocate for themselves
- Monitor their progress

Problems for People with Common Learning Disabilities

A person with average or above average intelligence who has an information processing problem, characterized by uneven abilities and difficulties in one or more areas, is identified as having a learning disability. There is a wide range of specific symptoms that a learning-disabled person grapples with. Here are some common categories:

Dyslexia	Difficulty with a reading task
Dysgraphia	Difficulty with a writing task
Dyscalculia	Difficulty with calculations and processing math facts
Attention Deficit	Difficulty concentrating, focusing on a task, and organizing work; highly distractable
Auditory Perception	Difficulty processing information that is heard; remembering verbal instruction; concentrating on lectures; hearing sounds over background noises; taking telephone messages
Visual Perception	Difficulty processing information that is seen; observing differences between objects; copying details from a blackboard; completing exams or computerized forms
Language Deficit	Difficulty articulating words; retrieving words; distinguishing various tenses of verbs
Memory Deficit	Difficulty remembering facts, figures, dates, multiplication tables, and so on
Reasoning Deficit	Difficulty thinking in an orderly manner; prioritizing or sequencing; transferring a known skill to a new task
Spatial Organization	Difficulty perceiving directions: left from right, up from down, ahead from behind
Social Skills	Difficulty understanding body language, facial expressions, and auditory cues, such as voice tone; difficulty accepting criticism and dealing with humor

How the Problem Shows Up in School

Language Processing and Reading Problems

You will have difficulty with word problems, but may comfortably handle them if the problems are read to you.

Quantitative Thinking Problems

You may have trouble *organizing* and *sequencing information* or have difficulty with verbal-spatial areas, such as estimating distances or distinguishing differences in sizes, shapes, and amounts. *Kinesthetic* difficulties may present themselves in the area of copying from a textbook or a blackboard with accuracy. *Visual processing* difficulties may also surface, as when numbers and letters are reversed and confused or it is difficult even to remember what a number or a letter should look like.

It is very likely that you may experience one or many of the following behaviors:

_____ Difficulty understanding what has been said

_____ Difficulty expressing yourself

_____ Leaving out or adding words when you read aloud

_____ Forgetting things very easily

_____ Losing or leaving your belongings

_____ Feeling generally disorganized

_____ Having trouble meeting schedules and deadlines

_____ Misreading body language and feeling left out of social situations

_____ Making inappropriate and impulsive comments

_____ Feeling angry and frustrated as you try to struggle with daily routines

_____ Problems with writing, spelling, reading, foreign languages, and basic math concepts

_____ Poor eye-hand coordination

_____ Finding it hard to listen closely and pay attention

_____ Needing to have directions and instructions repeated

_____ Having trouble being on time

_____ Finding it hard to stay on task and complete the task

_____ Difficulty remembering names and dates

One or more of these characteristics, that are commonly found in college students with a learning disability, may be areas that you need help with. Make sure your college learning center is aware of your specific learning problem. Check off those that you feel pertain to you.

Reading skills

_____ Slow reading rate

_____ Poor comprehension

_____ Limited ability to retain the material you've read

_____ Trouble identifying the main theme

_____ Difficulty with new vocabulary

Written language skills

_____ Many spelling errors

_____ Poor use of grammar

_____ Incomplete or run-on sentences

_____ Slow writing

_____ Poor penmanship

_____ Unable to copy accurately from a blackboard or textbook

_____ Difficulty organizing your ideas

Oral language skills

_____ Unable to concentrate on the lecturer

_____ Unable to understand the lecturer

_____ Difficulty expressing your ideas

_____ Unable to relate a story or event in the proper sequence

_____ Difficulty using proper grammar when you are speaking

Math skills

_____ Little or no mastery of basic math facts

_____ Number reversals

_____ Confusion with the basic math symbols

_____ Copying problems incorrectly

_____ Unable to understand abstract concepts

_____ Difficulty reasoning clearly

Organization and study skills

_____ Trouble getting projects started

_____ Time management problems

_____ Short attention span, with a need for frequent re-focusing

_____ Difficulty with asking for clarification of material in class

_____ Highly distractible

_____ Unable to work independently

_____ Difficulty following oral and written directions

_____ Easily forgetting content of lectures and class discussions

_____ Lack of organization in written material

_____ Poor use of library resources

_____ Difficulty in establishing priorities

_____ Difficulty in taking notes

_____ Unable to organize information into categories

_____ Difficulty in summarizing information

_____ Can't reduce tasks to smaller, manageable units

_____ Difficulty in meeting deadlines

Social skills

_____ Poor reading of social cues, such as facial expressions and body language

_____ Difficulty in meeting other young adults and maintaining relationships

_____ Difficulty in living and working cooperatively, which can result in roommate and dorm tensions

_____ Inability to make eye contact

_____ Mood swings and impulsive or inappropriate behavior

_____ Poor self-advocacy skills

_____ Difficulty accepting criticism

_____ Easily frustrated

_____ Difficulty empathizing with others

_____ Difficulty understanding cause-and-effect relationships

_____ Low self-esteem and self-confidence

We certainly never expect our family or friends to do *all* things equally well. Nevertheless, many people make the assumption that a college student will perform in both academic and social areas with equal ease. While many students can, many others cannot. You are now in the wonderful position of being able to take advantage of the special programs and services that will assist and support you throughout your college years.

Having a learning disability simply means that you will need to compensate for a range of diverse problems. While there are no cures for a learning disability, there are strategies and coping mechanisms that offer alternate ways for you to learn and grow. Special education professionals believe that responsive education is the most appropriate strategy.

Across the United States, students with learning disabilities arrive at college with exactly the same goals as the other students:

- To broaden their knowledge of the world
- To explore interests and new fields
- To develop career goals
- To prepare for independent living
- To make a contribution to society

There are now students with learning disabilities on every major campus in the country. Colleges are making great strides in sensitizing the college community to the needs of the learning disabled. This includes providing training sessions for staff and faculty to teach them more about students with learning disabilities, or workshops and panels for the general student body to raise campus awareness and promote the acceptance of individual differences.

Self-Advocacy

Many students with learning disabilities still choose not to disclose their disability and struggle through the system on their own. But given the changing attitudes, students who can acknowledge their limitations have greater opportunities to get assistance in every area of need and can aim for success in college.

Your own ability to talk about the limits of your learning disability with someone who can be helpful is called **self-advocacy**. To become an advocate for your needs you must:

- Have specific knowledge of your own strengths and limitations
- Be able to describe them specifically and discuss whatever accommodations you will need

For example, practice itemizing your needs to someone in this manner: "I can do _____ quite well, but I have trouble with _____ and I will need the following accommodation— _____." Unlike high school, where parents frequently intervened for you, you will now need to know what you need and how to get it. An accommodation simply is any assistance, service, or strategy that will help you cope with or compensate for your learning disability.

Take care that you don't thwart your own success. You must not:

- Hope to get by without the accommodations that you need

- Be unwilling to learn new skills and coping strategies

- Be stubborn and inflexible about your accommodation demands—be willing to negotiate and change if it's necessary and the solution will work for you

You already know that you will need to struggle to master some areas that others handle with ease. Take advantage of the opportunity to do so with the supports you need. There are trained people and services ready to help you. **Be determined to succeed**!

"Getting students to use the LD services available on their campuses is crucial. Those who take the first step to find out what is available are always glad they did. The requirements of college coursework can contain real surprises and students are often in trouble before they know it. My plea to students is to work with the LD staff sooner rather than later."

Dr. Irene Buchman
Director of Educational Skills

Summary: Learning Disabilities

A learning disability:

- Affects the use or understanding of language

- Has no external or physical indications

- Causes ongoing problems in learning basic skills

- Is not the result of emotional or environmental problems
- Is an internal deficit in people with average to above average intelligence
- Is generally defined as a significant difference between achievement and overall intelligence

6

Accommodations: Strategies and Special Services

Although your learning disability may affect the *way* in which you learn, it certainly does not affect your intellectual capacity. Fortunately, more and more teaching faculty and college administrators are developing ways to offer students with learning disabilities the chance to succeed in college.

The most common challenges for learning-disabled college students are:

- The ability to read texts and research materials
- The use of organizational skills for essay writing
- The integration of lecture material for note taking

Campus Accommodations

Most college courses have traditionally consisted of textbook-centered lectures. However, if college instructors are willing to learn more about learning disabilities and various learning styles, they could expand their own teaching styles. For example, some students with learning disabilities will thrive in a discussion format. An oral presentation, rather than the standard term paper, may better reflect their knowledge of the topic. The effort and preparation is just as challenging, yet this option can offer a way of compensating for a writing disability.

Unlike a student in a wheelchair or one with a seeing eye dog, faculty members have no way of knowing—until *you* offer the information—that you have difficulties in processing information, organizing material, or retrieving information, or that you may learn very differently than other students.

Perhaps you think clearly and logically, but just cannot construct a paragraph or write an essay. Perhaps you are articulate and in good command of the language, but are unable to read college-level texts or understand a group of directions.

A student with learning disabilities generally needs to dedicate much more time and effort to achieve the results of the more traditional learner. It can easily take two or three times longer to complete the same task, be it finishing an exam or completing a homework assignment. And while more energy and effort is needed, frustration levels can also rise. Finishing the project, completing the course, and getting the degree takes a great deal of perseverance and motivation.

Auditory and visual deficits are common for many with learning disabilities. When a student misperceives what is heard, he or she will not comprehend or understand the information. Others will have problems reversing or omitting letters, numbers, or words. Memory deficits are another common problem area. Complex oral directions may be hard to remember, as are dates, distances, weights and sizes. Because of this long- and short-term auditory and visual memory deficit, many people with learning disabilities are very poor spellers. This can be complicated further by the inconsistent behavior of the individual. Disabling features, in mild to severe forms, appear, seem to disappear, and then reappear without warning or any apparent pattern.

There are certain situations in which common problems arise, depending on the nature of the learning disability:

Oral language difficulties

- Attending long lectures
- Remembering the correct sequence of events

- Understanding rapidly spoken conversations
- Pronouncing complex words

Reading difficulties

- Comprehending what is read
- Retaining information from read materials
- Identifying the main theme or the important points
- Phonics problems
- Skipping words or losing your place on the page

Written difficulties

- Poor handwriting
- Scanty essays and written projects
- Spelling errors, letter and number reversals, words omitted or added
- Incorrect sentence structure
- Poorly developed ideas and no organization

Math difficulties

- Understanding word problems
- Copying problems accurately
- Reversing or transposing numbers
- Remembering the steps in an equation or a formula
- Computation deficits

Study skills difficulties

- Organizing and budgeting time
- Initiating and completing tasks
- Note taking and outlining material
- Following directions and instructions
- Taking more time than is available to complete your assignments

Social difficulties

- Low tolerance of frustration
- Giving up easily
- Poor response to pressure
- Poor sense of humor
- No sense of "body space": talking too loud, standing too close to others
- Inability to accurately "read" the facial cues or body language of others

What Faculty Members Can Do to Help

Be aware of these commonly available measures that many faculty offer and recommend:

- The college's learning resource center
- Talking tools, such as the Franklin Speller or Kurzweil Personal Reader (a computer that views printed material with an optical scanner and then reads it aloud to you)
- Learning disabilities specialists
- Tutoring help by professionals
- Peer tutors
- Note-takers
- Scribes (or writers for exams)
- Oral exams
- Distraction-free testing room
- Extended test time
- Use of calculators, dictionaries and spellcheckers during exams
- Books on tape
- Permission to tape record lectures

- Large-print exams
- Dictation services for those with severe reading deficits
- Franklin Speaking Dictionary, which provides 300,000 definitions, a spelling corrector, and a grammar handbook

Because your classroom instructor will see you at least once a week in class, and often more than that, he or she will become an important part of your life. It's vital that your instructors are familiar with the variety of strategies that benefit students with learning disabilities. They should be encouraged to:

- Make the class syllabus available several weeks before classes begin to allow you the opportunity to purchase books and begin the reading assignments
- Give all assignments in written format, as well as orally, clearly explaining all expectations and indicating the due dates
- Begin lectures with a review and overview of the topics that will be covered that day
- Be available during office hours to clarify material and respond to questions, and encourage this kind of contact with you
- Break down large assignments into smaller components
- Frequently ask students how they can facilitate their learning
- Make eye contact with every student
- Encourage questions and class discussion, and allow enough time for this
- Allow the use of tape recorders in class
- Slowly and clearly explain procedures in a sequential step-by-step manner
- Emphasize main ideas and key points frequently
- Aim for concise and clear instructions and sentences when designing questions for exams
- Review what a test will cover as well as the kind of test it will be: essay, short answers, or a combination of these

- Leave ample white space for margins on the test page so that students are not overwhelmed with information
- Give new directions on each section of the test as the format changes
- Encourage students to ask for a rephrasing of a test question if it seems unclear
- Allow students to clarify a test question in their own words as a means of checking their comprehension
- Speak clearly while facing the class and be alert to signs of confusion or frustration
- Repeat directions more then one time
- Leave wide margins for notes on handouts that are distributed
- Use a chalkboard or overhead projector, or highlight key ideas
- Eliminate or reduce the number of timed tests, which are of little educational value
- Allow oral or taped papers, projects, and presentations, in addition to written ones
- Search for quality rather than quantity in reports, homework, and projects
- Monitor the progress of students by giving frequent and specific feedback, so that improvement can be pinpointed
- Repeat, repeat, repeat
- Discuss with the class the value of study groups, which benefit *all* students
- Help interested students find study partners and organize study groups
- Provide examples of study questions for exams that show the test format that will be used
- Ask self-disclosing students how their learning can be enhanced
- Check to see if students understand a newly introduced concept by asking a student to volunteer to summarize or give an example of the concept

- Try to understand the impact of a learning disability on the life of a young adult
- Alert students to textbooks and other materials on tape
- Be sure students are aware of the special services offered on campus
- Let the class know the office hours schedule several times during each semester
- Keep in touch with the learning center, with the student's permission—the education specialists should know if the student is falling behind or needs additional support
- Facilitate the sharing of notes or arrange for a more formal note-taking service
- Praise, encourage, and nurture *all* students

What College Administrators Can Do to Help

- Familiarize faculty and staff with Section 504 requirements through workshops, presentations, panels, and conferences
- Encourage faculty and staff to develop policies and systems to respond to Section 504 and the needs of the learning disabled on the college campus
- Allow those guidelines to be widely circulated
- Develop a Center of Disabled Student Services and publicize the services and supports that are available
- Educate the faculty and staff about the nature of learning disabilities, focusing on the "hidden nature" aspect of the handicap
- Aim to sensitize all those who deal with students to eliminate myths and misconceptions
- Foster communication among service providers on campus
- Provide funds for memberships in professional organizations and attendance at appropriate conferences
- Allow students to carry light loads or part-time loads and to study during the summers to keep up

- Provide trained professionals who understand issues of low self-esteem, mild depression, performance and test anxiety, and similar issues that are common among those with learning disabilities
- Praise, encourage, and nurture *all* students

Other Materials

Treated Paper

Special paper is available for note-takers that could simplify the task, although traditional carbon paper is still available. Some people prefer to photocopy the notes of the note-taker, but that involves the chore of getting to and paying for the copying process. The specially treated noncarbon paper allows for two or even three clear copies. You should be able to order it from the college bookstore or from:

> The National Institute for the Deaf
> Rochester Institute of Technology Bookstore
> P.O. Box 9887
> Lomb Memorial Drive
> Rochester, NY 14623

Kurzweil Reading Machine

This handy unit scans and reads aloud English texts set in any one of 300 typefaces. It was originally designed for the visually impaired, but it is becoming more common as a helpful aid to students with learning disabilities. It makes books available for "reading" that have not yet been put on tape. It's most helpful for those who have good listening and comprehension skills.

Be prepared to learn to master this machine. It may take you a dozen or more hours to learn just how to operate the KRM. Check to see if your college or local library owns a unit before you invest in one. If you are interested, contact:

> Kurzweil Computer Products Inc.
> 185 Albany Street
> Cambridge, MA 07139

Summary: Accommodations for You to Consider

If you have difficulty with:

Consider the following:

Distractibility
- Work, study, or be tested in an isolated, distraction-free area

Getting organized
- Keep a list of things you need to do on a daily basis
- Keep a calendar for weekly, monthly, and long-term projects and due dates
- Learn to prioritize the most important tasks and decide which one or ones you will start
- Set realistic time limits for projects you begin and refer to them so you will know when you are behind on your schedule
- Ask for specific and detailed directions for tasks and projects you are unfamiliar with
- Attend a time management course or workshop

Writing legibly
- Use a word processor or a typewriter
- Try to give oral reports rather than written ones
- Dictate material to a note-taker or a scribe

Following written instructions
- Ask for a demonstration of what needs to be done
- Get oral instructions
- Tape record the instructions

Math computations
- Use a calculator
- Ask someone with good computational skills to check your work for errors

Spelling
- Use a dictionary

	• Use a spellchecker
	• Ask someone with strong spelling skills to check your work
Oral instructions	• Ask for written instructions
	• Ask for a demonstration of what needs to be done
	• Ask for instructions to be given in short, simple statements
	• Repeat those instructions to determine if you fully understand them
Lecture classes	• Tape record lectures and class discussions
	• Use a new tape for each lecture and clearly label it with the date, class, and subject
	• Listen to the tapes as soon after each lecture as possible
	• Ask for a note-taker or arrange for a classmate to share his or her notes each session
	• Arrange to sit in the front of the classroom and try to stay focused on the lecturer
	• Join a study group to review lectures and discuss key points and main concepts
Reading and comprehension	• Locate a distraction-free study space to do your reading
	• Use taped textbooks
	• Use a Kurzweil Reading Machine
	• Check with the college bookstore for textbook notes or outlines for your required readings
	• Request a peer tutor

Test-taking

- Request a distraction-free exam room
- Arrange for the use of a word processor, calculator, dictionary, or any other aids you will want to use during an exam
- Have the exam read to you, or ask the professor to have it on tape
- Ask for extended time
- Have a scribe record your answers
- Plan an alternate format, such as an oral response rather than a typical written response to the test questions

---

Faculty, staff and administrators should be encouraged to learn more about the needs of students with learning disabilities and to keep abreast of current innovations that will be helpful to you, as well as current legislation that will work in your behalf.

7

Financial Aid for College Students

One of the greatest concerns of students and parents is how to pay for the cost of a college education. Tuition is an issue for every family. But don't let costs stop you from fulfilling your college plans! You and your family are responsible for your college expenses, but **you can get financial help if you qualify**!

That help is called **financial aid**. It is simply a system of assistance to help meet your education expenses. College costs include:

- Tuition
- Room and board
- Transportation
- Books and supplies
- Activities fees
- Personal expenses

Money is available from the state and federal government, as well as directly from the college and from private sources.

Locating Financial Aid

Student financial aid comes in several forms:

Grants.   Grants encompass money that does not have to be paid back. Grants are generally based on your financial need.

Scholarships.   This is also money that does not have to be paid back. Scholarships are often based on your performance through test scores, grades, class standings, achievement in sports, the arts, leadership, or community service.

Loans.   A loan is money that you borrow and agree to repay with interest. Student loans are available from the government at low interest rates, or sometimes at no interest at all. Loans are also available to your parents to assist them in paying for your college costs.

Work-Study.   Work-study jobs are usually on the college campus. These jobs enable you to earn a portion of your college costs.

Financial aid is given to you based on the demonstrated need in the difference between college costs and what you and your family can reasonably afford. Important factors are:

- Your *parents'* income and assets
- *Your* income and assets

A system called **needs analysis** measures your family's financial situation and determines an estimated family contribution. **Financial need** is defined as the difference between your family's contribution and the costs of college.

The formula for determining financial need is:

Expenses –	Family Contribution =	Need
• Tuition and fees	• Amount the family and/or	• This
• Books and supplies	student is expected to	need
• Room and board	contribute toward the cost	may be
• Transportation	of your college education	met by a
• Personal expenses	• Contribution is determined	financial
• Expenses related to	by income, assets, social	aid
your learning disability	security, benefits, welfare	package.
• Study abroad costs, etc.	payments, etc.	

Although getting through the financial aid maze requires a bit of work, the rewards surely make the time and energy invested worthwhile. With college costs on the rise, grants and loans may be the only way you can consider a two- or four-year program, unless you are fortunate enough to be eligible for scholarship funds. At one time it was even reasonable to think of working your way through college. Given current tuition rates, that may no longer be easy to do.

The good news is that there is financial aid money available and just about every college in the country offers a financial aid program. At last count, more than seven million undergraduates were receiving some form of financial assistance, mostly from the federal government.

It is in your best interest to become aware of the financial aid process. Read all financial aid materials sent to you by the schools you are considering. Attend workshops and seminars on this topic at College Fairs and College Nights. Unless you are an independent student, you will need to enlist your parents' support to get all of the needed tax documents and wage statements together. *The key is to remember to file on time and not miss deadlines!*

Applying for Financial Aid

It's best to file financial aid forms when you mail your admissions application, rather than wait until you are accepted. *Earlier* is definitely better than later. It allows enough time for the financial aid professionals to determine if you qualify and what financial aid package they are prepared to put together for you. It may take as long as six weeks before a decision is given to you, so timing is important if your decision on what college to attend depends on the aid you will be offered.

In your last year of high school, you should complete the application form for Federal Student Aid (FAFSA or Needs Analysis Form), which you can get at your high school guidance office or from local college financial aid offices. This form will ask for detailed information about your family's income and their assets for the current calendar year. In addition, most private schools will want you to complete their own financial aid questionnaire as well.

To process your family's information, the federal government formula is used to calculate the "expected family contribution," which is the amount of money the government assumes your family can contribute toward your education, based on income and assets.

- To meet college bills, the government's aid formula assumes that families can contribute as much as 47 percent of after-tax income.

- Students are expected to contribute 35% of their own assets to meet school costs. Because of this, having a large savings account or other assets in your name may not be an advantage at this time.

- As your family's ability to contribute will remain the same no matter what college you attend, your financial need will be determined by the fees and costs at the college you select.

Don't dismiss the idea of scholarships. They are awarded each year by government agencies, corporations, union, civic groups, and other organizations. Most tend to be relatively small amounts, usually within the $500–$1,000 range. If you are granted a need-based financial aid package, your college may deduct the scholarship amount from their aid package to you. Your best bet for scholarship information will come from a college financial aid office or your high school guidance or college counselor. Check with your parents about whether their employer or union has a scholarship program for children of employees. Use your school or local library to utilize reference sources, such as *The College Financial Aid Annual*. Your library should have listings of state and private sources of financial aid. The United Negro College Fund provides details about scholarships and financial aid programs at its 41 member schools. You can write for information to:

> The United Negro College Fund
> c/o Education Services Department
> 500 East 62nd Street
> New York City, N.Y. 10021

A free pamphlet available from the federal government explains:

- Federal Pell Grants
- Federal Supplemental Educational Opportunity Grants (SEOG)
- Federal work-study (FW-S)
- Federal Perkins Loans
- Federal Family Education Loans (FFEL), including federal Stafford Loans and federal PLUS Loans.

Write for a free copy of *The Student Guide: Federal Aid From The U.S. Department of Education*:

> Federal Student Aid Fact Sheet
> Box 84
> Washington, D.C. 20044

You can also call (800) 433-3242 or (800) 730-8913.

Applying For Financial Aid is a small newspaper which covers basic information about the process. Sample calculations and sources of financial aid are described. You should find copies in any college financial aid office, but you can also call or write for a free copy to:

> ACT
> P.O. Box 168
> Iowa City, IA 52243
> (319) 337-1040

Colleges want to help families who are financially unable to cover education costs, but not those families who are *unwilling* to do so. Students who knowingly give false information on financial aid forms may face stiff penalties and fines, and even jail.

Call upon the professionals in the college's financial aid office to give you guidance in completing the forms if they seem somewhat confusing to you. It pays to do this, and it may make financing your college education less burdensome. You must be a wise consumer. Shop around until you feel you have received a good financial package. Colleges want to attract students and are becoming more innovative in their awards as they grapple with:

- Declining applicant pool
- Increasing competition for students
- Rising costs of a college education

Avoiding Financial Aid Errors

Don't Assume That You Are Not Eligible

Many students just do not bother to apply because they know other students in a similar financial situation who were turned down. Some students are convinced that they will be ruled ineligible because their family owns their own home or earns more than $75,000 per year. In truth, there is no actual income cutoff. The aid system is a rather complex formula that takes a great many factors into account, such as:

- Size of family
- Number of other children in college
- Age of the oldest parent

It is possible for a family with an income of $125,000 or more to receive financial aid. It is *definitely* worthwhile for you to apply.

Don't Miss Deadlines

It's important for you to apply for financial aid at the same time that you apply for admission. There is only a limited amount of financial aid dollars available, and priority is given to those students who meet the deadlines. Most students think that the time to apply for aid is after they have been accepted, but in many cases this is far too late to take advantage of the college's resources. Students who file early will beat you to the funds!

Don't Ignore the Process

Don't fill out the forms and then forget about them. Make photocopies of everything that you send and check with the school to ensure that all your records and necessary information have been received and are complete. You can also ask if there is anything else that is needed to improve your application. Be assertive and keep track of what has been received and what is still needed to meet each college's requirement.

Don't Assume That You Can't Negotiate a Better Financial Aid Package

It's not necessarily the college's job to maximize your financial aid package. And it is certainly possible to try to negotiate a *better* financial aid package. If you've had a bigger award offer from a comparable school, you can tell the financial aid counselor that a more generous package was in fact offered by college X. Be honest, as you may be asked to show proof of that award. Remember that schools can change the amount of an award. The first offer they make is not always their best or final offer.

Don't Reject Student Loans When Part of a Financial Aid Package

Student loans are a good deal for you and compare favorably with other options. Need-based student loans, such as Perkins Loans and subsidized Stafford Loans, charge *no* interest and do not require you to repay the principal until you leave school.

Don't Assume That Outside Scholarships Are Always a Better Deal

Scholarships from private foundations, unions, and agencies actually represent less than 1 percent of all financial aid available. You may not gain much if the college reduces your award by the amount of the scholarship you get from the outside source. If you *do* qualify for an outside scholarship, convince the college to reduce the loan and work-study portions of their package to you, rather than the grant money.

Financial Aid Essentials

Apply for aid every year you are in college.   Even if you are not eligible, you should take the time to apply. Changes in your family's financial situation may affect your eligibility.

Get the correct application forms.   Some colleges use their own form, others use a more standardized form. Deal with the financial aid officers at colleges to which you have applied, or ask your high school counselor to get the proper papers that you will need.

Assemble everything you will need.

- End-of-year pay stubs and W-2 forms for you or your parents.

- Records of last year's untaxed income for social security, social services, and veteran's administration.

- Last year's federal and state income tax forms for you and your parents.

- Social security numbers for you and your parents.

- Bank account balances, lists of stocks, bonds, and other assets, estimated value of real estate, *not including your own home.*

Meet all deadlines.   Check with each school to find out what their deadline for filing an application is. To meet the filing deadlines, you can use estimated income if your tax forms have not been completed. Use estimated income figures from W-2 forms or end-of-year pay stubs. *Fill out the applications accurately, completely, and on time!*

Attend financial aid workshops.   These sessions can offer valuable information and assistance in the filing procedure. Speak with your high school counselor or local financial aid officer to get dates and locations of these workshops. And be sure to ask questions. Financial aid professionals have the latest information and are interested in helping you.

Keep your own records.   Make copies of your signed and dated application forms before you send them off. Be sure they are signed by you. In some cases, your parents' signatures may also be needed. You can take the extra step of mailing your applications by certified mail. If you request a return receipt, you will be mailed a signed receipt by the school's processing center.

Financial Aid Calendar

When you are a junior in high school, it will be helpful to:

_____ Check out financial aid opportunities with your guidance counselor.

_____ Attend financial aid presentations at College Fairs or College Nights.

_____ Write to colleges of interest for applications and financial aid forms.

_____ Start to gather financial information you will need to complete the forms.

When you are a senior in high school:

_____ Get proper financial forms for the schools you will apply to.

_____ Use income and financial information you gathered last year or get this year's estimated tax information.

_____ Complete financial aid forms.

_____ Mail forms as soon as possible *after January 1*. Forms with a postmark before January 1st will be considered invalid.

_____ Check application deadlines for each school.

_____ Keep a list of the dates you sent out the completed forms. You should get acknowledgment in about six weeks, indicating your form was received.

_____ You will get a Student Aid Report (SAR) in another six weeks. This should be sent to the financial aid offices of your college choices *immediately*.

_____ If you get no response within eight weeks, call the Student Aid Center listed on the aid form or in the institutional booklet.

_____ Keep in touch with each school's financial aid office while your application is being processed.

"My best advice is to apply for Financial Aid. However, you must actively participate in the process by:
- Reading all materials sent to you by the Financial Aid office
- Applying early and observing deadlines
- Making sure each application is complete and accurate
- Making an appointment with a Financial Aid counselor if you have questions
- Persevere"

Lucille Higgins
Director of Financial Aid

8

The Rights of Students with Learning Disabilities

Public schools are required by law to provide learning-disabled students with an appropriate education. School systems all across the nation now make every effort to comply with the law. Learn what benefits and services you are entitled to receive. If you feel that your rights are not being met, you can contact your state's Learning Disabilities Association (LDA) chapter for guidance and direction. Experienced volunteers who are familiar with Special Education laws and programs are available to act as a resource or refer you to other resources that can advocate for you.

Know Your Rights

The provisions of the law are intended to *equalize* opportunities for the learning-disabled student and are *never* intended to lower academic standards or program requirements. The Vocational Rehabilitation Act of 1973 was important legislation. Section 504 is a basic civil rights provision aimed at putting an end to the discrimination against the handicapped. It says:

"No otherwise qualified handicapped individual in the United States shall solely by reason of his handicap, be excluded from the participation in, be denied the benefits of, or be subjected to discrimination under any program or activity receiving federal financial assistance."

This law includes **specific learning disabilities**. For college students, the word "qualified" refers to a handicapped person who meets the academic and technical standards required for admission to or participation in an educational program or activity.

This means that Section 504 of the law requires that all college faculty, administration, and staff know that:

- You cannot be excluded from a course, a major, or a program solely based on your handicap

- Academic accommodations or modifications *must* be made as long as they do not change course objectives

- Modifications, substitutions, or waivers of a course, a major, or degree requirements may be necessary to meet the needs of some learning-disabled students

- Flexibility in the time needed to complete a degree or a program may have to be allowed

Also, under the provisions of Section 504, colleges and universities may not:

- Make pre-admission inquiries as to whether or not an applicant is disabled

- Use admission tests that inadequately measure the academic qualifications of disabled students because special provisions were not made for them

- Limit the number of students with disabilities that are admitted

- Establish policies that may adversely affect disabled students

- Counsel a disabled student toward a more restrictive career

- Measure achievement using standards that adversely discriminate against a student with a disability

- Exclude a disabled student who is qualified from any course of study

- Limit financial assistance to any student with a disability

And you need to know that learning-disabled students may require a range of special services, which might include:

- Basic skill remediation
- Tutoring services
- Developing test-taking skills
- Developing study skills
- Note-takers
- Readers
- A distraction-free room for exams
- Extended time for tests and assignments
- Permission to tape textbooks and lectures
- Academic advisement
- Program modifications such as a reduced course load each semester
- Clarification of test questions
- Exams read and answered orally
- Flexible time allowed for the completion of a degree
- Substitution of specific courses

Once you indicate your needs, it is the responsibility of the college to be sure that appropriate aids and supports are available to you at the proper time. If the accommodations you need don't present an undue financial or administrative strain on the college— or require fundamental changes in program requirements, **the college must pay for the costs of those accommodations**. For instance, if you needed class notes from your lectures, the college's Special Education Center might decide that an equivalent level of access to that material could be gotten with a tape recorder or a student note-taker. The college may select the less expensive choice and provide it, as long as it is effective for you.

The college or university must demonstrate a **good faith** effort in providing you with effective accommodations. The institution does not have to provide the most expensive or comprehensive accommodations you request. But the college must be ready to defend its choices for you based on documentation that you provide.

If you feel you would like to learn more about the Vocational Rehabilitation Act of 1973 (Section 504), you can write to:

> U.S. Department of Education
> Office of Special Education and Rehabilitation Services
> Washington, DC 20202

In colleges and universities, federal regulations mandate "reasonable accommodation" for all students with learning disabilities. For you to qualify under Section 504 you must have a diagnosed learning disability and be able to submit that documentation to the school after you are admitted. When thinking about your choice of school, be aware that state universities receive federal and state funds. They must abide by all legislation that relates to the student with learning disabilities and are obliged to make "reasonable accommodations" for you. Some private colleges may not be as willing or as able to serve your individual needs, based on their particular funding arrangements.

What to Do, What to Expect

- You should be prepared to apply for needed accommodations and present appropriate documentation.
- An institution must have policies and procedures for dealing with accommodation requests.
- You will need to take some responsibility for securing your accommodation and reporting if it is not satisfactory.
- If you request accommodations that are not adequate, you must ask for different and more effective accommodations.
- A grievance procedure for resolving such requests must be in place in the school.
- Course materials must be available in alternate media at the beginning of the term.
- Note-taking methods must be flexible and the institution must provide tape recorders, computers, and so on.

- There must be no harassment or retaliation as a result of your requests.

You Know Best!

As a prospective college student, you are best equipped to identify your own educational needs. You must be prepared to determine the programs and services you want to be put in place for you. This will happen after you've consulted with your parents, high school counselors, therapists, or other special education professionals. You have the choice of identifying and requesting any accommodations or services necessary to compensate for your disability.

Therefore, it is your responsibility to notify the proper office or appropriate person on campus of your disability and of the types of accommodations you will need. Or you can work with the college's Special Education or Learning Center to determine exactly what adjustments will be decided upon for you. **You must make your request at the proper time to allow the institution to respond by providing the accommodation**.

Securing academic adjustments, whether it's a reduced course load, modified testing, or the use of some aids, will allow you the opportunity to be a self-advocate and offer you the chance to work with faculty members and special education professionals on the campus. Always keep in mind that this is a "team approach" rather than an adversarial one. Although academic self-sufficiency is your aim, the ultimate goal is to develop your responsibility and independence.

The skills that you learn in post-high school settings *do* transfer to other settings, such as a work environment. As you develop an understanding of your limitations and some knowledge of the use of effective learning strategies, you will be preparing for your future. You *can* learn to be better prepared for college and for the world of work.

Documenting Your Learning Disability

You will need to provide any institution with documentation of your learning disability, so be sure you have whatever paperwork your high school can give you. Section 504 does not require a college to pay for a diagnostic evaluation to document your learning disability. But if your school disputes the evaluation you give them, the school may have to pay for a second, updated evaluation if they feel they want it. Although Section 504 does put responsibility on you, the learning-disabled student, *once documentation of your learning disability is complete and turned over to the college, it is then the responsibility of the college to respond to your request for services.* Keep in mind that the provision of services is required *only if you inform the college of your disability and request specific services.*

Standardized Tests

At the turn of the century, each university had its own admissions test. This was generally in the form of an essay and often had to be completed in Latin. The College Board was formed in 1901, and the SAT was designed to help college admissions counselors make choices among applicants by referring to their test results, along with the students' high school records.

The SAT, which measures math and verbal skills, is now given to almost two million high school students each year. Most colleges require students to submit SAT scores as part of the application process. In 1994 the testing service began to give a revised SAT exam. (The revision of the test actually came about when a student representing a class of disabled students felt their rights were being violated with the traditional test. That student's disability required extra time to complete a written exam, because she could not read as fast as many other students.) The changes reflect more of what is currently taught in the classroom. The new test has been designed to place greater emphasis on reading comprehension, and also reduces the number of multiple choice questions in the math section. And, for the first time, you can solve math problems with the aid of a calculator. *The aim of the test is to predict success in college.*

It is likely that you will be faced with two typical admissions policies:

- Open Admissions—requiring a high school diploma or the equivalent

- Regular Admissions—requiring a high school diploma or the equivalent, your rank and g.p.a. in your high school class, and acceptable scores on a designated, standardized test

The law mandates that institutions accept scores, such as SAT and ACT, from tests administered under non-standard conditions. You may also be asked to give additional information on your strong areas. This may add weight to your admissions application.

You can also offer colleges your psycho-educational and diagnostic reports. Learning disabilities specialists and special education professionals on campus should review and interpret these materials with the admissions counselors and be a part of the decision-making process.

The Educational Testing Service and The College Board provide students with learning disabilities with a variety of SAT editions of the test, including a cassette version. You may also elect to have additional testing time when taking a regular edition of the SAT. If you require extra time or other special accommodations, there are several dates on which you could take the new version of the test.

Preparing for the Tests

Section 504 has been amended to place more pressure on school districts to help achieve compliance with the law.

In your senior year:

- Get help in studying and preparing for SAT and ACT exams, *if* you plan to take them.

- Arrange accommodations *in advance* of the day of the test, depending on your need (for example, untimed test, the use of a reader or a scribe). Be clear about exactly what will be needed.

- If your high school guidance counselor cannot provide you with details, contact the agencies directly for information about special accommodations for college entrance exams.

For the SAT exam, contact:

> Admissions Testing Program
> Services for the Handicapped Students
> P.O. Box 6226
> Princeton, New Jersey 08541-6226
> (609) 771-7600

For the ACT exam, contact:

> ACT Assessment
> Test Administration
> P.O. Box 168
> Iowa City, Iowa 52243
> (319) 337-1332

9

Visiting a College Campus

Earlier we discussed the importance of visiting the colleges that you are interested in. It is definitely a **trip worth taking**. In this chapter we explore the campus visit in greater detail.

Seeing It for Yourself

Just about every school you contact will present an appealing image through colorful literature and attractive videotapes. However, *there is no substitute for a personal visit*. You will find that most schools, whether they are large or small, public or private, are eager to have you tour their campus. They want to show you their special features and unique programs in the hopes of "selling" both you and your family on their school. Many colleges and universities involve current students in helping with admissions tours. The students are often selected because they are very involved with campus life and will present a positive image of their campus. Think twice about a college that appears to discourage campus visits or makes you feel as though it will be complicated or even unnecessary.

Seriously think about visiting each campus in which you have a fairly strong interest. Carefully select those that appear to be real possibilities for you, and that can be visited within your family's travel budget. If you can visit four or five different schools, that's great. Up to six campuses is excellent. If you are considering more than that, you may need to spend more time reviewing brochures and program offerings and narrow down the field to a more manageable number. Because of limited time and money, most students visit local schools and plan on just one or two excursions to colleges that are a distance from home. By the way, don't plan on any college reimbursing you for your travel expenses, even if you are a scholarship student.

The time of each campus visit will vary, depending upon your own time schedule and that of the school. You should plan on at least a half day visit to get the information you need, but you should ideally try to allow yourself at least one full day. If at all possible, spending a night in the dorm and eating a meal or snack in the dining hall will give you a real chance to get the spirit and flavor of the student body and the institution. At a minimum, your campus visit should include the following:

- Meeting with an admissions representative
- Campus and facilities tour
- Contact with Special Education faculty or Learning Center professionals
- Meeting with the department chairperson or faculty member of the program you are considering

Make the Most of Your Visit

The ideal time to visit is while classes are still in session and students and faculty are still on the campus. Many schools plan a **Visiting Week** or a **Preview Week** just for this reason. These events might allow you and your parents to see the campus, stay in the dormitory, attend classes, and meet with faculty members and advisors. They are ideal opportunities to gain a sense of the campus. Not every campus organizes such programs. You may need to work with an admissions counselor to set up your visit and discuss which programs or classes you should be observing and which faculty or administrators you should be meeting.

Just dropping in without a scheduled appointment will probably not be productive, particularly if you've bothered traveling from a distance. The people you need to meet with may not be available at the time or the day you are on campus. A scheduled personal visit will allow you to get the feel of the campus and each program in a way that can't be duplicated by looking at catalogs or student handbooks.

Visiting During the Summer

You may want to visit during the summer, when the college's summer school is in session. It may even be a somewhat more relaxed time on the campus than during the academic year. You may also have more time to spend on the campus than during the academic year, and the admissions counselors and department chairpersons might also be more available. You'll need to set this visit up in advance to ensure that you don't miss people you want to see, who may be on vacation during summer months.

Arrange for a meeting with the department chairperson of the program that interests you, as well as with the admissions counselor. It is important for you to meet with the Special Education Coordinator or head of the Learning Skills Center. This will allow you to gain some insight into the philosophy of the program and how the department operates. Spend enough time reviewing the college catalog so that you are prepared with questions or concerns that need to be discussed.

Be sure you look appropriate. This is not the right time for tank tops and cut-off jeans. Save that for the beach. Neat and appropriate dress will help you feel a bit more confident, and you won't stand out like a tourist on the campus. Try to be yourself without being concerned about impressing anyone. But remember: in addition to your viewing the school, the people you meet with are also taking a look at you.

Try to spend some time in the cafeteria and the dining halls. Plan on eating at least one meal or snack in the lounge areas. This will quickly give you a sense of the quality of the food service. It would also be a good time to meet with the dietitian if you have any particular dietary needs. Look to see how varied, healthful, and attractively presented the food is. Note how clean the area is and how relaxed and comfortable the students seem.

Read everything. Check posters and bulletin boards to learn what is happening on campus and off. See what school events are publicized and look for details about weekend programs, social events, parties, apartments to rent or share, books and furniture for sale, and so on. Read copies of the school newspaper on file in the library. Review recent editions to give you a sense of the issues that were or still are important on campus, and how those issues are being handled.

Don't feel shy about taking notes during your visit, especially if you are viewing several schools on the same trip. Jot down impressions, and items you liked or found annoying so that you end up with an accurate record. As with any important decision, your choice will not be based on a single factor. Plan for the visit, ask questions, research the information you and your parents will need to know. Your college experience will certainly color the direction your future will take, so invest the time to review all the choices open to you. You'll gain a great deal from each visit, including the sense that certain schools will not work for you.

Visitation Weekends

If a school of your choice offers a visitation weekend that is convenient for you to attend, *do it*! You can often participate in such events as early as your junior year in high school. The idea of spending a weekend on a campus at a modest fee (usually in the $25–$35 range) with some meals included, will truly allow you to see the school in an informal way and come away with a real sense of that particular campus. You'll have a chance to talk with a variety of students, administrators, and faculty—maybe even alumni. You'll also get the program information you need. Best of all, you'll have an opportunity to see just how well-organized the institution is and how they treat students and prospective students. Sometimes you will even be able to attend athletic and social events being held on the campus.

There's usually a schedule for parents and family, while you and other students get more involved with "student-related" activities. If at all possible, don't let a visitation weekend pass by without taking advantage of it.

Checklist: Making the Most of a Campus Visit

_____ Contact the Admissions Office to arrange your visit well in advance of your preferred visit dates.

_____ Ask about special campus tours and visitation weekends for high school students and their families.

_____ Plan for times when the college is in session and all facilities are open.

_____ Meet with faculty and department chairpersons of the programs that interest you.

_____ Set up a meeting with the head of the Learning Center or coordinator of the Special Education Program. Be sure to tour those facilities.

_____ A wonderful source of information will come from the students on the campus. _Ask questions_. Talk to as many students as you can to find out about everything from the cafeteria food to student government issues. You'll always get very subjective responses, but you can be put on the alert to any problem areas that may exist.

_____ Note the level of enthusiasm and interest as you talk with students and staff members.

_____ If school is in session when you visit, ask permission to sit in on several classes.

_____ If possible, arrange an overnight stay in the dorm.

_____ Eat in one or more of the dining halls and snack and lounge areas.

_____ Check out the Student Activities areas and look for student lounges and relaxation and social spots.

_____ Find out about special interest groups: student government, the radio or TV station, student publications, the Drama Society, the Hiking Club, and so on.

_____ Tour facilities of special interest to you. If Computer Science is a program you'll be taking, make sure the hardware in the computer lab is state-of-the-art.

_____ Scan bulletin boards to get a sense of weekend and mid-week activities: athletic, social, and cultural.

_____ Visit the gym, medical offices, career counseling, and job placement area.

_____ Meet with Student Life counselors, dormitory personnel, academic advisors, medical professionals, and so on. These people will be a part of your support team and you need to be assured that they are welcoming and responsive.

_____ A library visit is important to determine how well stocked and current the volumes are. Make sure the program of your choice is well-represented with books, magazines, and scholarly journals.

_____ Take notes. Jot down facts, as well as your feelings and impressions as you view the campus and meet its representatives.

_____ The Alumni Office can share names of past graduates in your local area. You can contact them at your convenience after the visit to ask for their feelings about the school and its programs.

Regardless of what your choice will be—a four-year college in an urban center or a smaller community college in a rural area—you will want to be in a setting that is comfortable. You are the best gauge of whether or not a campus is a good match for you. But no matter how ideal the setting is in meeting your *image* of what a college campus should look like, it *must* have the services and supports to meet your needs. Only then is it clearly the right setting for you.

Aim to make each campus visit more than just a chance to see another school or take a trip. Allow each visit to serve as a real exploration of where you may be living and learning. And don't forget to ask yourself this important question: **Can you picture yourself on this campus for the next two or four years?**

Think about What You Want to Gain from Your College Experience

Decide on the issues that are important to you—not the ones that friends or siblings value.

- Coed or single-sex school?
- Large, small, or mid-size?
- Urban or rural?
- Two- or four-year college?
- Close to home or far away?
- Comprehensive support program or limited services?

You need answers to these questions before you can select the school that will meet all or most of your needs and make your final decision. Start your research early. Keep notes to compare the benefits and shortcomings of each of the schools you read about and visit.

Investigate the student housing as thoroughly as possible.

- Determine dorm fees as well as off-campus housing rates.
- Ask if all freshman *must* live on campus.
- How is the billing handled? Is it paid in installments or is the entire amount due before the semester starts?
- Is a security deposit required?
- How is the security deposit refunded?
- How are damages assessed and billed?
- Must you have a roommate or can you choose to live alone?
- Will you share a bathroom or are private bathrooms available?
- Is there one meal plan for everyone or can you have a choice of plans?
- Are meals a fixed price or can you buy things a la carte?
- What do you think of the food service?
- Does it meet your dietary needs?

- What kind of residence would you prefer? Coed or single sex? Small (25–200), medium size (200–400), or large (over 400)?

- Are theme floors available? Non-smoking, by major or program, international students, graduate students, married/family floor?

- What is available in the residence hall? TV or video room, study areas, laundry facilities, lounges, fitness center, computer area?

- What is provided in the typical residence hall room? Basics usually include a single bed, dresser, lamp, desk, chair, and closet. Ask if you can add extra lighting, smoke detectors, a mini-refrigerator, or toaster oven.

- Can you bring a telephone, answering machine, microwave, TV and stereo?

- Is there room to store luggage, bikes, sportsgear, or exercise equipment?

- Are there any restrictions on making your space more attractive? Can you paint, put up curtains, posters and prints, hang plants inside windows?

- Are there laundry facilities? Can you rent linens and small appliances?

- What are the procedures if there are problems with roommates?

- Can you request a change of rooms or of roommates? Is there a fee?

- When do residence halls open and close?

- Can you stay on when school is closed for winter or spring breaks? Do you pay additionally for this?

- Do you sign a contract to live in a residence hall? What are the terms? What happens if you want to live off campus? What are the penalties for cancelling your contract?

This is the time to be super-organized. Begin to keep a file for each school of interest to you. Either highlight what each school is asking for when you complete their application, or make your own list of information that you have to supply to that institution. Be aware of financial aid deadlines.

10

The Admissions Process

You have the same dreams and goals as any other high school student—so searching for the college that will work best for you requires many of the same steps used by students all across America. Some additional work on your part will assure that your particular needs are met. Students with learning disabilities who apply to private institutions should be prepared to be invited in for a personal admissions interview. You and your parents will have a chance to meet with an admissions counselor to discuss and explore the school's programs and services. This is all a part of a learning and decision-making process, to help determine if you can thrive, and *excel,* on that campus.

The Admissions Interview

Although this is a stressful process, view it as an opportunity to learn as much as possible about what the college can offer you. At the same time, the admissions professionals will be learning more about you and your specific needs. The goal for everyone is to determine how good a match the college and the program of your choice are for you. Be prepared to ask and answer questions. Use the admissions interview time to your best advantage by carefully thinking about what you want to find out. Be prepared to discuss specific information about yourself that you want the admissions counselor to know and take into account. The institution's programs and facilities will form the basis of your support system. Your success in college may well depend upon the kind and quality of such services, many of which will be offered at no additional cost to you. More individualized offerings, such as diagnostic testing, individual counseling, and tutoring may be available, but only on a fee-for-service basis. You'll need to ask about this.

Standardized Tests

Standardized tests are one of several standards that a college admissions officer uses as a criteria for acceptance. Your high school class standing and overall average are important information as well. Letters of recommendation that attest to your diligence and academic commitment will also be helpful in rounding out a picture of you as a prospective college student. Your written essay and personal interview give further weight to your willingness to accept the challenge of education after high school.

If your SAT scores represent a significant problem for you, don't despair. Not all colleges and universities require admissions testing. Many small colleges are pleased to consider students who may bring achievements in sports or art areas rather than solid academic scores. Some schools offer academic support to assist you along the way. You can always look to community colleges as an alternative once you have your high school diploma. In fact, if you do take some courses at a community college and get good grades in those classes, you could establish a suitable academic record, which can help you transfer to the school of your choice. The admissions for transfer students is generally based on your college course records instead of college admissions test scores.

Be aware that SAT and ACT exams can be taken under *nonstandard* conditions, including:

- Extended time
- Large-print editions

- The use of a reader
- The use of an assistant to mark your answer sheet for you

You will need to contact your high school guidance counselor for details on special testing and to make your request far in advance of the actual test date. You can take these tests several times for practice purposes and you can sign up for a preparation course.

In addition to high school academic records, you will probably be asked to submit:

- Intelligence test scores
- Untimed SAT scores
- Written statements of recommendation from high school teachers

These items will help the admissions professionals determine if you are ready to function on the college level. Although tests often *underestimate* a student's potential, the WAIS-R is frequently an accepted indicator of the level of academic and social abilities and of achievement. Many schools routinely request a WAIS-R score as part of their admissions process.

Ask if the school requires a psycho-educational evaluation. Some schools like to do their own testing and some schools require no test reports at all. Don't be put off by any institution that wants your test results. They are likely to use that information to help arrange the best possible supports for you.

Let the admissions counselor you meet with know that you acknowledge and accept your learning differences. Interviewers want to honestly hear you acknowledge what you cannot do and what you will need help with, as well as hear you stress your abilities. Define yourself in terms of what you *can* do. And be prepared to articulate:

- The services you need
- How you learn best
- Any aids or accommodations that will be helpful

Most importantly, be ready to show your enthusiasm and convey your seriousness and determination to succeed in college.

Highly motivated students are what admissions counselors are searching for!

Admission to Special Programs

Special learning disabilities programs may require a separate admissions process after you complete the admission to the school. A special education professor is generally available to help coordinate your program for you and offer academic advisement, as well as arrange for tutoring or individual counseling. It is also likely that your counselor will act as your advocate on campus. It is recommended that students with learning disabilities identify themselves early in the admissions process. *This choice is your own and strictly a personal one.* There is *never* any mention of this fact in your transcript. Your learning disability should not prevent you from entering a school if you meet all of the school's requirements. But it is very important for you to take advantage of any or all services available, as well as have an advocate or a support group on campus for you to rely upon.

By now you know that federal law demands that colleges and universities provide special assistance for students with learning disabilities, although it does not require that schools maintain a special office on campus. In some schools, informal services are provided through the Office of the Dean of Students or the Dean of Student Life. You will also find growing numbers of campuses with separate departments or offices that manage the programs and services for you.

If a school that interests you has no office or center specifically designated to assist students with learning disabilities, it is important to be able to clearly explain your limitations to a campus representative and determine if the help you need will be available. You might want to consider writing a brief statement that outlines your particular needs that you could include along with your college admissions application. Design it to describe whatever accommodations you need, but make certain that it indicates your strong points and areas of interest.

You'll discover that not every school will ask for a personal interview. You would still be wise to arrange for one. You can use the time to convey to the admissions representative your eagerness to become a college student and your level of motivation. It's the perfect time to discuss your strengths as well as your shortcomings and how you plan to take advantage of whatever services the college has to offer. Some schools admit limited numbers in their learning disabilities programs, so it is important for you to be as prepared as possible to present yourself as a serious and determined candidate, ready to handle the challenge of college-level work.

Questions You Should Be Prepared to Answer

Become familiar with the following list of commonly asked admissions questions. Prepare responses. Practice answering so that you are comfortable and relaxed in your presentation. Discuss possible answers with your parents or teachers and counselors until you find the response that makes sense for you. Get into a role-playing situation where you enlist someone to ask you questions.

- Describe your past school experiences.
- In what academic areas have you been most successful?
- Which areas have been more difficult for you?
- What kinds of accommodations have you needed?
- Describe your specific learning problem.
- When was it diagnosed?
- Talk about the limitations you have and the areas you would like to strengthen.
- What supports or accommodations will you need in college?
- Have you taken any college prep courses in high school? Which ones?
- Have you thought about career goals? What are they?
- Did you get involved in extra-curricular activities? Which ones?
- Were you involved in any sports programs? Which ones?
- Have you had any experience doing volunteer work or community service?

- What are your hobbies or special areas of interest?
- Have you ever held a job? What kind of work did you do? Did you like it? What did you learn from it?
- Why are you interested in going to college?
- What interests you about this particular college?
- What do you feel you could contribute if you were admitted?

Questions to Consider Asking the Admissions Counselor

Prepare the questions you might want to ask the admissions officer. Chances are your interviewer will be pleased that you have given some thought to so many issues. Not all of the questions listed may apply to your situation. Ask those that have meaning for you and think of others that are important for you to get responses to.

- How many students with learning disabilities are enrolled?
- Are they full- or part-time students?
- How many live in the dorms? How many are commuter students?
- Can you describe the typical student with learning disabilities? Male or female? Age ranges?
- How many students use the support services?
- Describe the special programs or services. Are they remedial, psychological, or compensatory?
- Is a special admissions application required for those programs? How does it differ from the regular application process?
- What test reports will I be asked for?
- How recent should test reports and scores be?
- Are IEPs from my high school needed?
- What is your policy regarding SAT or ACT exams? Can they be waived?

- If I am accepted to the college, will that mean automatic acceptance into your learning disabilities program?
- Are there additional fees for the LD services offered on campus? What are they?
- What is the student/professional ratio of the Learning Disabilities Center?
- Describe the backgrounds of the director and the staff.
- Are they certified in Special Education areas?
- Is the director or head of the LD center available on a full-time basis?
- Is there a staff of other professionals that is adequate to meet the needs for the number of students with learning disabilities?
- Will a specific staff member be assigned to work with me? For how long?
- How often does the typical LD student use the services?
- Who will be my academic advisor?
- Will I take specific LD track courses, or be in regular courses and get support services?
- If there are LD courses, is it for the entire program or just for certain subjects?
- Are the LD courses I take credit bearing?
- Will they count towards graduation? Are they required?
- Are there courses that I cannot take because I will be in the LD program?
- Is there a standard package of services or will you develop an individual plan for me?
- Who determines what services I receive?
- Will my test scores be used to plan or modify my program?
- Is there an orientation program or seminar for students with learning disabilities? Is it mandatory? Does it cost extra? Do I take it for credit?
- What is the graduation rate for students with learning disabilities?

- How does this compare with the general student population?

- Do you follow up to learn what your LD students have done since graduation?

- How active is the college's placement and career counseling department? What was last year's placement rate?

- Could I talk with one or two currently enrolled LD students?

- Could I have the names of several LD grads so that I could speak with them?

- When will I have to declare a major?

- Will I lose credits if I decide to switch majors?

- Are the courses I've taken in high school relevant to the major I'm considering?

- What grades must I maintain to stay in the program?

- Describe your tutoring program. Am I eligible? Is it free?

- Are there peer tutors or trained professionals? If there are peer tutors, how are they trained and supervised?

- Is it subject matter tutoring, or learning strategies?

- Is the tutoring one-on-one or in groups? What size are the groups?

- Would I work with the same tutor for each session? For each subject?

- Are testing and diagnostic evaluations available on campus? What are the fees?

- If it's not available, could you recommend me to an agency?

- Is psychological counseling available? What does it cost?

- What financial packages are available?

- At what point can I work with a career counselor?

- Is there a center or office that coordinates all services for students with learning disabilities or are they offered in individual offices such as counseling, placement, and so on?

- Are student support groups available for the LD student on campus? Who runs the groups?

- What topics are generally covered?

- How big are the groups and how often do they meet?

- If there are no such groups, is there a way for LD students to get to know each other?

- Can you talk about typical accommodations that are made for LD students?

- Are these accommodations available in classrooms and lecture halls, test-taking situations, and in study halls and the library?

- Are course substitutions allowed?

- Can I consider a reduced courseload each semester?

- Can I participate in internship or work-study opportunities in that program to get actual industry experience?

- Will I be able to change my major if it is not the right one for me?

- When does the school need to know my final decision about choice of major or program?

- Can I meet with that program's chairperson and faculty members?

- Can I arrange to stay overnight on campus?

- What percentage of entering freshmen graduate from the college?

- What is the placement rate for graduates of this program?

- How available are faculty members to students? Do they have regular office hours?

- How many credits must be taken to be considered a full-time student?

- How many credits do I need to take to be eligible for financial aid?

- If I am interested in the _____ program, what will my courses be in my first year? In the second year?

- Can I get a two-year degree and then consider moving into a four-year program?

Making Programs More Accessible

There are various steps that can be taken to make a program more accessible to you.

Reduced Courseload

For some students with learning disabilities, just carrying fewer than the standard 17–18 course credits each term may be the only adjustment needed. It simply means spending more time completing the program until all course and credit requirements are met. Chances are no one will ever question exactly how long it took you to get your college degree. The more important questions are likely to be: Did you graduate? When? Be sure to find out if the services that you need will be available to you regardless of how many courses you take, so that you do not risk your eligibility for them. In most colleges with a specific program for the learning disabled, a part-time program or a light course load is encouraged. A typical semester load usually means five to six courses. If you begin with three or four, you give yourself a good opportunity to adjust to the college setting and work out a study schedule that suits you.

The Learning Center, Special Education Center, and Student Services Office

If you know you require a variety of supports and services, it's important to look at schools with a central office on campus to arrange and coordinate, as well as monitor, those offerings. The services may range from minimal to extensive, but it is essential to have a designated staff of professionals (or at least one professional in a smaller setting) dedicated to the concerns of the learning disabled. When you visit, find out where that office or center is and who is in charge of it. The best arrangement is for you and your parents to meet with that person or a representative of the center to learn how it can help meet your needs.

Ask the person you meet with to arrange for you to talk to other students with learning disabilities on the campus. You will quickly be able to gauge how helpful and how heavily used the services are. Also ask about the department in which you plan to study. You should know how responsive the chairperson and faculty are when requests for special accommodations are made.

Study Skills and Remedial Course Work

Exposure to a study skills course or workshop can give you effective and organized ways to approach your courses. Everything from establishing a study schedule to note taking or preparing for exams can be learned. In some programs, you will be told you must take remedial courses in English or Math because of your high school grades. Approach this as a second chance to master the subject. Remedial courses may not count towards the credit you'll need for your degree. Check with your academic advisor to determine this.

Readers, Note-Takers, and Scribes

If you have a severe reading problem, ask whether paid or volunteer readers are available to read texts and any other materials to you.

If you have serious difficulty writing, or getting ideas and concepts in your note taking, you may profit from the assistance of a note-taker. He or she will actually go to your classes with you and take notes during the lectures and class discussions. You must remember that this person will accompany you to class, *not go instead of you.* You could also make arrangements to photocopy the notes of another student in the class who is a thorough note-taker. This can be done informally once you get to know others in your courses.

A scribe will actually write for you during your tests or whenever you need to work on your term papers, reports or other projects. They are trained *not* to ask you questions or make comments to you, so they don't clarify or enhance or even change your answers in any way.

Class Outlines

Some schools urge faculty members who teach basic courses to entering students to put together a daily outline for each lecture.

The outline gives you an overview of what will be covered at each session. This is a great help to your note taking and is helpful to the entire class, not just those with learning disabilities.

Non-Traditional Testing

Various testing methods should be available to you. Extending the amount of time allowed for an exam may be of help to some. For others, a distraction-free test room, working with a reader or a scribe, and using an electronic speller, calculator, word processor, computer or a dictionary may be helpful.

Computer Center

Computers have thoroughly changed the way the world shares information. Students who have difficulties with spelling or writing find that computers are very important and helpful. Any college program that you are investigating should have a strong computer center and include plans to train students in the use of computers.

Counseling Services

Adolescence is tough enough without the burden of a learning problem. A professional counseling staff can be valuable in helping you develop during your time in college. Meeting with a trained counselor on an individual basis can help you accept the limitations of your learning disability and enhance your self-esteem.

Help with stress, time management, study and test-taking skills, and other coping strategies are frequently offered in workshops and may even be open to all students, as these are common areas that most entering students need to master. A strong counseling center might be considered vital to the success of many college students.

Student Support Groups

More and more, support groups are cropping up on college campuses. Student support groups can be important in dealing with issues ranging from differences with your roommates to explaining your specific learning problem to your professors. Through discussion, and often with role playing, you may develop strategies that will allow you to take new risks, and receive group feedback and support.

A wide range of such services is now fairly common on more and more college campuses, so it is very likely that you can select the particular accommodations you need. Be sure to find out if the special services you require are available to you as part of your tuition, or if additional fees will be involved. You'll need to know about all these costs when you compare the schools and their programs.

Putting Together the Application

A typical admissions package may request the following:

- An application form (a sample form follows)
- An essay or personal statement from you
- Your official high school transcript

Transcripts must be sent by your high school, stamped with the school's official seal. They should list the courses you have taken, and the dates, credits or units, and grades. Transcripts must also indicate courses repeated or failed. Honors will also be noted as well as your numerical rank in your graduating class.

Schools will also request recommendations by your counselor, college advisor, or senior-year teachers. The recommendations should indicate your extracurricular achievements, as well as your motivation to learn and your interest in meeting and overcoming your educational challenges.

Admissions Essays

If you need to write an essay as part of your admissions application requirement, keep these tips in mind:

- Your college essay makes an important difference in how

your application is viewed. Students often spend less time on the essay than on other parts of the application form. If you skimp on the time you invest in the essay, you lose the opportunity to make yourself stand out. After all, you cannot change your exam score or your class rank, but you can aim for a unique or memorable essay.

- Try to customize what you write to fit the college's image. Be sure to include some items in the essay that can indicate to the admissions counselor that you know about and understand the mission and philosophy of that particular school.

- If you've made a campus visit, write about your impressions and what you learned about the campus or a particular program that impressed you.

- You can use the essay to explain what some of your learning difficulties are and how you have learned to overcome them, but this must be done in a *positive* manner.

- If the essay form requests that you respond to specific questions, check to see that you have done so and that you have not wandered off the topics.

- Your writing sample must be as good as possible. Proofread it and then have someone else check it for grammar and spelling errors. Keep it neat and watch out for typos.

- Don't be afraid to tailor it to what you think the college is all about. It should also give the reader a glimpse into what *you* are all about. You can ask a teacher or a counselor for their suggestions and comments. Rework it until you feel it's a good reflection of who you are and you are completely satisfied with the final product. It could make you stand out from the rest!

It's a National Trend

To make life even easier for those who are computer literate, colleges from New York to California now allow you to apply for admissions electronically. Officials are interested in reducing the stress of massive amounts of paperwork and realize how convenient filing electronically is for you, as well as for those who actually process the applications.

Sample Admissions Application

Application for Admission

_____　_____
LAST NAME　　　　　　　　　　　　　　　　　FIRST NAME

_____
SOCIAL SECURITY NUMBER　　　　　　DATE OF BIRTH　　　　　　SEX

_____
PERMANENT MAILING ADDRESS

_____
CITY　　　　　　　　　　　　　　　STATE　　ZIP　　TELEPHONE

CITIZENSHIP: ____ U.S. ____ Permanent Resident U.S.

　　　　　　　　____ Other Country _____ Visa #

I am applying for admission in ____ September ____ January
_____ (year) as a

____ freshman ____ transfer student ____ international student

I am interested in the ___ Associate Degree (first two years)

　　　　　　　　　　　　___ Bachelor's Degree (third & fourth years)

I am interested in the following programs: _____

　　　　　　　　　　　　　　　　　　　_____ or

　　　　　　　　　　　　　　　　　　____ undeclared major

I will be a candidate for financial aid ____ yes ____ no

I am interested in on-campus housing ____ yes ____ no

I am interested in ____ full-time or ____ part-time programs

continued

List the most recent schools you have attended:

_____

school name and address   dates attended

_____

name of guidance counselor   indicate program taken

If you have ACT or SAT scores indicate:

_____ verbal score _____ math score _____ date taken

ACADEMIC HONORS: Describe any scholastic honors you have
been awarded.

_____

_____

_____

EXTRACURRICULAR ACTIVITIES: List extracurricular involvement or community service.

_____

_____

_____

WORK EXPERIENCE: Indicate any work experience, paid or un-
paid, and include dates and type of work.

_____

_____

_____

FAMILY INFORMATION:

_____   _____

FATHER'S NAME   MOTHER'S NAME

_____   _____

ADDRESS   ADDRESS

_____   _____

continued

ARE YOU LIVING WITH YOUR _____ MOTHER _____ FATHER

If accepted, who will be responsible for tuition payments? _____

PERSONAL STATEMENT:
Write a brief essay about one of the following topics:
- Why you are interested in getting a college education.
- What interests you about this college.
- What your career goals and plans for the future are.
- Describe yourself and your family.
- Write about an important personal achievement.

Even if you don't have a PC at home, ExPAN, a nationwide network created by The College Board, will allow you to use computers available in high school guidance offices in more than 450 schools across the country.

If You Are Rejected

Don't panic. It can happen to anyone. You may want to consider finding an interim or temporary job locally, while you pursue your alternatives.

- Begin to research other less competitive schools
- Consider colleges with rolling admissions where you will get a speedy response to your admissions application
- Apply to them for the next semester
- Enroll in a post-graduate year at a LD prep school to build up your skills while you have the time
- Consider programs at your local community college
- Take college courses for credit during the summer to begin to build up some transfer credits while you get a taste of college.

Summary: Getting into the *Right* School

Your selection of the school that will suit you best depends upon a variety of factors, but should follow some guidelines:

- Determine your academic limitations and the educational supports and services you will need.
- Identify the schools that indicate they can provide the services you require and that also offer a program in an area of interest to you.
- Research and investigate the schools that seem most likely to deliver the supports you need.
- Consider tuition, fees, distance, and the overall feeling of comfort you were left with after your campus visits—before you make your decision!

11

Off to College

With high school almost behind you, the challenge of college now lies ahead. It's a brand new start for you. Try not to dwell on school issues and problems that may have plagued you in the past. You can be ready to face your exciting future with a clean slate, whether you were a high achiever or had a string of disappointments in high school. Naturally, you will be anxious about fitting in and understanding life on a college campus, whether you are a commuter or a residential student. Realize that just about every freshman or transfer student is experiencing similar concerns. Remember that each department in the college is there to help you succeed and get through their program. Educators understand that your academic success is as important as your social success, and they are available to assist you when you ask for help.

Preparing for College: Summer Courses

You may have the opportunity to take a college course during the summer before beginning your first semester in college. If it fits in with your plans, consider doing so. You will not only have a head start on earning credits, but can slowly adapt to the demands of college life and get an overview of the college while dealing with just a single course or two. It will be much easier getting adjusted before the fall semester crowd arrives.

You can familiarize yourself with the campus, the student center, the library and other resources. If you decide to take a course in a college other than the one you enrolled in (such as your local community college), you will still get a look at what goes on in the world of higher education. Remember that summer session work is often condensed, so material may be presented at a faster pace than during the regular semester and homework assignments may feel burdensome. This is because you are having daily classes rather than one or two per week, as happens during the typical semester.

Think of this new beginning as an opportunity to show the best side of yourself.

- Put information you have learned about yourself and how you learn best—including your stronger and weaker areas—to use.

- Take advantage of every service and support that works for you.

- Explore the new world around you to take the best advantage of college life.

- Initiate new relationships. Introduce yourself and reach out to classmates, floormates in your dorm, staff personnel, faculty, and administrators.

- Take the initiative and sign up for campus events, such as counseling, career planning, freshman orientation events, leadership workshops, and student government activities. Any of these events will put you in touch with other students. Student clubs and special interest groups can also help you break the ice and allow you to deal with issues and programs of real interest to you.

"Participate in student activities: experience new opportunities, learn necessary life skills, develop new friendships, and have a ball doing it!"

Dr. Nancy Grossman
Director of Student Life

- Become an active participant, even if you involve yourself in just one activity per semester. You will begin to make connections with students and faculty members who may be important to you during your college years.

- Learn to master the skills that are important to your success. Understanding how to manage your time is critical. Unless you plan on being a commuter student, family members will no longer be available to remind you of deadlines and help you set priorities. It will be up to you to get to classes on time, keep appointments, and hand in assignments and projects on time.

- Work to improve your study skills so that you can truly focus on the content of every course without being sidetracked by note-taking, research, and test-taking concerns.

- Try to develop a positive attitude about your college experience. You've come a long way. You can always reduce your courseload and improve your study habits for greater ease and success in future semesters. Be confident about the strong areas of your performance and try not to focus on your limitations. Concentrate on one successful semester at a time, rather than feeling overwhelmed at the prospect of four long years of college.

- Allow yourself to enjoy dorm life and the social and cultural exposure you will have. It's time to reach out and join clubs and groups that interest you. Participate in areas you've never before experienced. Of course, the trick is to do this while keeping the balance of enough attention to your studies while enjoying the spectrum of residential campus life. Your academic success must always be your first priority.

- Attempt to link up with someone on campus. It is important for you to feel connected to another person at the college, whether it is a dorm resident, classmate, instructor, or counselor. This will allow you to air your concerns about the frustrations and annoyances that are part of every student's life away from home. If you are isolated and feel alone, minor situations will begin to feel like major concerns. Trading stories of your dissatisfactions with others can help minimize them and allow you to realize that everyone goes through the process of adjusting to a new and different environment.

Getting Ready for the Academic Year

You can do some **homework** before your program actually starts. This will give you a sense of confidence and familiarity with your new campus setting that will ease the jitters of your arrival.

- Get a headstart on learning about campus facilities. If possible, make arrangements to be on the campus for an early orientation.

- Contact the Learning Disabilities or the Support Services Center well before classes begin to introduce yourself and make your needs known. It will be helpful for you to learn the names of the people you will be working with, such as the head of the center, counselors, and tutors. Keep a list of those names, room numbers, telephone numbers, and office hours.

- Set up appointments to meet with the Dean of Student Life or with faculty advisors. Discuss your particular needs and expectations so that everyone is clear about what accommodations need to be provided for you.

- If there is no particular support program on campus, meet with the chairpersons of the various departments you will take courses in. You might want to include the Dean of Student Life. A joint meeting would alert the appropriate faculty to your situation. You can discuss the campus resources that are best suited to your needs.

- Meet with the counselors, tutors, and advisors you have been assigned to. Start to collect any handouts, such as manuals, student handbooks, guidebooks, or outlines and review them.

- Check out the college bookstore. It's always less crowded and less confusing *before* registration takes place. Bring the list of textbooks and supplies you'll need to buy. Shop also for the calendars and other aids to keep you organized. If this task seems overwhelming, request an escort from the Learning Center who can accompany you and show you the ropes. Find out if you can pay by credit card, cash, or check and if you will need to show your student I.D.

- Meet with instructors before classes begin if you can. Make them aware of your interest in doing your best. Use the meeting time to describe any special requirements, such as getting permission to tape record lectures or take untimed tests. In the interest of being courteous, you can alert them to your needs, although it is likely that the Learning Center counselor or your advisor will have already done so with your permission. You can arrange for your Learning Center contact to talk to each of your professors on your behalf. This should only happen *with your consent*. You might also want to consider writing a brief note to each faculty member to introduce yourself and indicate whatever accommodation you'd like to request.

- Remember that you must learn to function as your own advocate on campus. People can only be responsive to your needs if they are aware of them. Arrange to ask for all the accommodations you need and actively participate in any decisions relating to your education. Seek the help that is offered as soon and as often as you need it!

- For help in a hurry, keep a master list of essential telephone numbers in your purse or wallet. It should include the dorm resident assistant or a friend in the dorm; professors or tutors you might need to call to discuss an assignment or project with; your contact in the Learning Center; and anyone else who you think might help in a crisis. We all face minor emergencies from time to time.

Making the Transition to College Life

Your life in college will be different from anything you have yet known.

- You will be away from home, old friends, family, and familiar surroundings.

- You alone will be in charge of getting yourself to class on time.

- Classes will be larger and longer than the classes in high school.

- You will need to do a lot of reading.

- You will be asked to write a lot of papers.

- You will have many new responsibilities.
- You will need to manage your time wisely.
- You will have to budget your money.
- You will need to make new friends.
- Dorm life will be less private than home life.

Along with all of these new and sometimes scary things, you will also be starting a new and thrilling experience that will be an important part of your young adult years.

Don't forget to bring these essential items:

- A copy of your birth certificate or other ID
- Your social security number
- Copies of any special testing, high school reports, or evaluations that provide details of your abilities and the services that you require
- Personal computer with a spellchecker or a Franklin Speller
- Dictionary and thesaurus
- Typewriter
- Highlighters, pens, pencils, stapler, tape, clips
- Tape recorder with a supply of blank tapes
- Book bag
- Daily calendar and weekly or monthly calendar for your study area
- Assignment book, notepads
- Calculator

Although many of these supplies are readily available at any campus bookstore, you'll have less to think about if you have them at your fingertips as you unpack.

12

Handling Difficult Issues

We *all* deal with unpleasant and often difficult situations throughout our lives. You will face a variety of ups and downs in your new role as a college student. You *can* learn to manage each new situation as well as possible. You will even learn to grow as a result of handling some difficult issues.

Handling Criticism

Although we all might agree in theory that feedback can be helpful to us, few of us actually *want* to be criticized. We spend a great deal of time and energy denying or dismissing it. Perhaps it's too much like our earliest memories of being scolded by our parents or other family members. So we protect ourselves by responding defensively to criticism in some common ways.

- **With anger**—By trying to convince the person who is being critical that "I'm right and you're wrong."

- **By withdrawing**—By trying to avoid the person who is being critical.

- **With passive-aggressive behavior**—By doing something that you think will upset or anger your critic, but without direct confrontation.

- **By perfectionism**—By attempting to be super-competent to avoid any more criticism.

Once involved with behavior of this kind, it's more than likely that you will completely miss some important information that your critic may have given to you but that you are unable to really hear. Whether it comes from an instructor or a roommate, there really are productive ways to cope with criticism. The important thing is to learn to feel less threatened by the criticism and to use the criticism constructively, for your own growth.

You may be able to change your usual response to criticism by:

- **Becoming more aware of your own distortions**—Before you get angry and upset by hearing the critical feedback, try not to react. Take some time to think about exactly what was said to you. Try to separate your feelings and your self-esteem from the actual content of the interchange. Listen closely for the real message. It may be important for you to hear.

- **Behaving more effectively**—Instead of falling back on your old and traditional responses, pay more attention to the message in the criticism. If any of it—even a very small part—is legitimate, acknowledge it! You can simply state that it's accurate and that you agree with the criticism without being defensive. If you think only a small part of the criticism is valid, say so. You do not have to be in 100 percent agreement with your critic. And you should never acknowledge something you honestly do *not* feel is valid for you, just to calm someone down or to keep the peace.

Try to get some more details about whatever behavior of yours is being criticized. You may have to ask some questions or probe a bit to get to the core of the issue and truly determine what's bothering your critic. The issue of handling criticism is a difficult one. But be aware that some people criticize others because they are angry, and really have little or no interest in improving a relationship with you. If you get the feeling that you are being attacked by someone who enjoys making you uncomfortable rather than trying to be helpful to you, steer clear of him or her as much as possible.

And don't brush off another's needs or feelings just because they are unlike your own. You may be able to fall asleep with your stereo blaring, but your roommate may not. You will both need to talk about some possible solutions that might be mutually acceptable.

Consider Brainstorming

Here's an opportunity to try to come up with solutions to a problem.

- Both of you jot down a list of possible solutions to the problem you're facing.

- Attempt to negotiate a reasonable solution by both suggesting ways you'd like to solve this issue. Continue to refine the resolution until you come to an agreement.

- Put the mutually agreed upon solution into operation for a specific amount of time—a weekend, a week, a month— whatever seems to make the most sense. Test it to find out if it *really* works for both parties before you do decide to settle on it. If it doesn't seem satisfactory, begin the process again, keeping in mind what you have learned about each other's needs and feelings.

Learning from Criticism

You can learn from criticism without necessarily having to *enjoy* it. It is often a source of educational and constructive feedback.

- **Take it seriously**—Pay attention to what is being said about you to assess how valid it is, before you shrug it off or become irritated.

- **Listen carefully**—Be open to hearing how others view your actions without feeling you need to criticize in return.

- **Accept it**—You'll never get any honest feedback if you make it hard for people to tell you their candid reactions to your behavior.

- **Be realistic**—Don't dismiss criticism or blow it out of proportion without carefully evaluating what is being said. You can then work on improving your behavior if it is warranted.

- **Don't be defensive**—You need to **hear what is being said to you**. Don't spend your time dreaming up excuses or apologies.

Handling Conflicts

No matter how compatible people seem, we all have different expectations and points of view. It's just not possible to have a relationship without some measure of conflict. But it *is* possible to control the level of conflict and prevent it from becoming a battle. Conflict is actually necessary. It helps us develop as we learn to handle it constructively.

Just as in handling criticism, it's important to think about conflict *before* you react. It will give you time to change your typical reaction patterns. It's helpful to look at how you traditionally respond when faced with conflict. Do you lose control and respond in ways that actually escalate the situation? To improve your reactions:

- Catch your breath
- Try to take a step back from the situation
- Try to think about what causes you to respond in the way you do

For example, if a friend delights in teasing you about your habits or behavior, it may really get to you and cause you to blow up. But if you step back from the situation and think about it without the anger you usually attach to it, it might help you to see how harmless the teasing is. It could still be very irritating to you, but perhaps you just need to ask that it be stopped because it's so annoying.

What you want to do is to attempt to control your behavior, even though your friend who initiated the teasing is the real culprit. But don't blame her or him for your reactions. That leads to your feeling "he made me angry" or "she's always getting me upset." What's more important is to forget about whose fault it is and attempt to improve the situation. Although it's never easy to change old and familiar behaviors, try to imagine yourself in charge of the situation. How would you respond? What would you say? You can rehearse in your mind how you might handle the difficult moment so that you will be better prepared when it happens. Best of all would be a chance to role play with a counselor or a friend you really trust who is aware of the conflict.

To allow for new ways of handling a situation, you'll need to:

- Understand why you feel and react in the way you typically do
- Acknowledge that you'd prefer to be in control of your behavior
- Take responsibility for your actions
- Agree to change your behavior

Putting Conflicts behind You

When you learn to resolve disagreements and find better ways to handle conflicts both large and small, you foster your own personal growth. Use such opportunities to collaborate and compromise, rather than ignore an issue or deny that there is a problem, which usually leads to escalating the issue and more conflict.

- **Talk about the problem**—All involved parties need to state their own perception of the issue.

- **Consider all solutions**—Come up with as many possibilities as you can. Don't judge them in advance as being "foolish" or "not workable."

- **Examine each solution**—Honestly review all those solutions that just might work. Toss out those that everyone involved agrees are not workable. Carefully discuss those solutions that may be truly difficult to put into practice or are just too expensive to consider.

- **Make a choice**—Select the one solution that is *most* acceptable to everyone involved in the problem. **Honesty is critical in this step**. Never agree to something that you cannot live with.

- **Take action**—Agree upon exactly who will be responsible for what actions, how, and when. Put this in writing if you feel it's necessary to remind yourselves of what was agreed upon. **All agreements must be honored**.

- **Review**—After an agreed upon time to test it, reevaluate how effective or satisfactory the solution is. If it's not working well, stay with it. If it's not, go back to the start and be open about the need to make it better!

Handling Complaints

There will always be a time when you feel the need to complain. So learn to express that complaint wisely, as opposed to whining, pouting, or blaming others.

- **Choose your starting point**—Begin with the person or the people directly involved. Avoid involving any others who are not part of the issue you need to voice your complaint about.

- **Gather your facts**—Try to present your information in a **neutral and objective manner**. State your case without casting blame on others. If this is too hard to do orally, you can put your facts in writing to help you when you make your presentation.

- **Go to the top if necessary**—If you feel you will not be getting satisfaction at the level you are dealing with, move up the ranks to that person's supervisor, a Dean of Students, or even the college president, if necessary. At this level, you may be asked to put your complaint in writing. An administrator may wait to review your written statement before meeting with you.

- **Aim for a specific resolution**—If it is agreed that the issue that you complained about will be looked into or corrected, establish exactly what will be changed: by what date, at what price, and at cost to whom? Don't settle for "things will be better" without knowing precisely how, what, and when the changes will occur.

- **Use your support system**—Research and take advantage of the counselors, advocates, or special groups on your campus who may be available to encourage you and lend their support to your issues. If legal steps are necessary, Legal Aid Society lawyers may be resources for you to investigate.

Don't make a career of complaining! But if you are convinced that you have a legitimate issue that needs to be corrected, don't be discouraged or give up without trying. Be committed to your cause. Your campus should have someone who can give you guidance and direction as you proceed.

13

Tips for College Success

Skills to Master

As a new college student, it will be critical for you to develop college-level study skills. Don't be overwhelmed by the wide array of skills that learning specialists feel are needed for academic success. They are listed here in order of importance. Some you may already have, and some you may need to work to acquire.

- Listening skills
- Ability to follow oral directions
- Ability to stay on task
- Knowing how to get help
- Ability to get started on projects and assignments
- Ability to complete work on time
- Work attack skills
- Math skills
- Reading comprehension
- Ability to follow written directions
- Ability to work independently

- Ability to be punctual
- Social skills
- Study skills
- Organizational skills
- Test-taking skills
- Spelling skills
- Writing skills
- Ability to work cooperatively in small groups
- Ability to copy accurately from the blackboard
- Note-taking skills

This might seem like a tall order, but rest assured that *no* college freshman enters with mastery of all these areas. Decide on which of these skill areas you feel most deficient in and want to improve. Then begin to focus on small measures that will start you thinking of new and better ways of handling a familiar situation. If workshops or seminars are offered on campus in skill-building areas, make sure you sign up and attend. Go as often as your time schedule allows so information can be reinforced.

Here are a group of social skills that will be as important for you to develop or improve:

- Reading facial expressions of others
- Understanding body language
- Appropriately responding when conversing
- Listening carefully
- Making eye contact
- Dealing with interpersonal issues
- Being sensitive to the feelings of others
- Accepting criticism

Learn How to Plan

You will most likely get reading lists, projects, and assignments for the entire semester in many of your courses. Begin to plan your time as soon as you receive those materials. Use your calendar to mark off the due date of *every exam, paper, and project*. This will enable you to see at a glance how heavy or light each week will be once you make all the entries. You can plan your daily routine once you know how much homework and study time is needed. Be realistic or you'll never accomplish much of what is on your daily agenda. **Always allow extra time for unplanned events** and build in free time each day for chores—or just to relax and catch your breath!

Keep your calendar in a visible spot so you see it every day! Your study area in your dorm room might be the best location.

Beating Procrastination

We *all* put off tasks and assignments for another day. But making a habit of this is the way to sabotage good time management.

- Do you often feel too busy and too overburdened?
- Are you distracted just as you're about to start a project?
- Do you feel as though you need to have every piece of information at your fingertips before you can think about making a decision?
- Does tomorrow always seem like the best time to start a new project?
- Are you often late for appointments and meetings, but always feel that you have a good excuse?
- Would you really prefer *not* to have to make any decisions?
- Do you feel that "immediately" or "as soon as possible" really means "whenever I can get around to it"?

If you answer YES to at least four of these questions, chances are you are a **procrastinator**.

A procrastinator will usually:

- Have difficulty starting and finishing projects
- Agree to do something and not do it
- Forget about promises that he or she made
- Start too many projects and rarely finish any of them

- Always have excuses for his or her behavior

It's hard to know what causes us to procrastinate, particularly when our procrastination centers around important issues, such as school, career, or social relationships. Here are some commonly accepted reasons:

- Fear of failing
- Not wanting to face a boring or difficult task
- Being burdened because of your poor time management
- Being unable to prioritize your work and assignments
- Feeling unsure about how to do the job
- Not thinking there is a real advantage to doing the job
- Resentment for having to do the job

Getting started will actually free you up once you take the first step! Fight the awful urge to put it off and do it later.

- Focus on the fact that you will do the job and complete it.
- Think of how nice it will be to get it over with.
- Think of how you'll like avoiding all the negative consequences of not doing the job, such as anger from people you're letting down and guilt from not completing what you need.
- Visualize how you can break down an overwhelming project into small, manageable steps.
- Set daily priorities that include handling those small steps by doing 15 or 20 minutes of work at a time.
- Work in a distraction-free space that's neat and organized.
- Have at hand the books or other materials you need for the project.
- Be reasonable in allowing ample time for each segment of the task.
- Set up a simple filing system so that you're never faced with stacks of paper waiting for you.
- Don't plunge in so intensively that you work or study around the clock or all weekend.

- Take the breaks and stretches that you need.

- Set a routine for yourself for more repetitive and dull tasks, such as paying all of your bills every Saturday morning.

- Learn to delegate parts of the project to others who can be helpful and who are self-starters.

- Think about whether you *really* have to do the entire job yourself or whether you can get someone to help you or pay someone to help you. This could cover everything from photocopying class notes to your weekly laundry.

- Consider the barter system, exchanging favors you don't mind doing with someone who will do what you can't or don't want to do.

- Don't be super-critical of all of your efforts. First drafts don't have to be perfect, but you do need to start them.

- Get the worst over first by trying to do the hardest or most irritating task, or the item that is due the earliest.

- Start with what you can to begin your assignment. Don't wait for every bit of information that you may not need until you're closer to the end of it.

- Always allow 15 to 20 minutes each day to review your mail and messages, review tomorrow's calendar, and set your priorities for the next day.

Terms You Need to Know in College

You will spare yourself a lot of confusion and worry if you become familiar with the language that college students need to understand.

Academic advisor.   The faculty member whose job it is to advise students on how to select their courses and plan their program each semester. It's important to do this with great care so that you meet all of the school's requirements for graduation and program completion.

Academic probation.   A serious warning to students that their academic progress is not satisfactory. The message is to straighten up or face failing the course or courses.

Admissions office.   The unit that reviews your school records and transcripts and interviews you to determine if you are acceptable for admittance to the school.

Baccalaureate degree or bachelor's degree.   The degree you are granted after completing four years or 128 credits of undergraduate studies.

Chairpersons.   The heads of the major departments, who administer those departments as well as teach.

Career counseling and placement center.   The department that will work with you in planning your career goals and assist you in preparing for your job search. They may offer specific job leads as well.

Campus life.   The office on campus that arranges and coordinates extracurricular activities, including student government, social programs, and cultural events.

Counseling center.   The unit that works with students who need assistance in dealing with personal issues. You will be served by professionally trained counselors who value confidentiality.

Co-op jobs.   Paid jobs in industry that relate to your course of study or major area.

Core curriculum.   The basic group of courses you must take to complete your program and graduate.

Dean.   A senior officer in the college. There may be several deans, each responsible for a different area, such as a Dean of Students, a Dean of Business Studies, or a Dean of Art and Design.

Drop/add.   For the first few weeks of each semester, all students can add to or drop courses from their program without a penalty, if done within a specified time.

Freshman orientation.   Programs designed to acquaint new students with campus life, rules, and regulations.

Health/medical services. The college's department for dealing with all minor health-related illness and injury; staffed by doctors, nurses and nurse practitioners.

Internship. A work experience in industry that is monitored by a faculty member. You may or may not be given school credit for the experience.

Major. The field of study you choose.

Midterm. Halfway through each semester, midterm tests are given so the instructor can gauge your progress. Sometimes reports or other projects are given instead of an exam.

Pass/fail. A rating in a course where you do not get the traditional letter grades of A, B, C, D or F, but receive a pass or fail on your transcript. Some colleges allow you to choose which system of grading you prefer.

President/chancellor. The head of your college or university.

Registrar. The office that is responsible for evaluating all records and grades and for issuing transcripts and diplomas.

Residence hall director. The person in charge of all dorms and residences on campus. The Director generally has a staff of Resident Advisors (RAs) who are students trained in dorm policies and will assist you with your concerns.

Semester. The breakdown of an academic year, usually totalling two or three semesters. In high school it was called a school term.

Student center. The area designated for relaxation and socializing. It usually includes a snack bar, recreation facility, and a bookstore.

Student government association. The voice of the student body run by the students. Get involved. Student government is a great opportunity for you to develop leadership skills or just be aware of campus issues that may affect student life.

Syllabus.   A printout of what readings, papers, and tests are due, and when, for the entire semester. It's often distributed at the beginning of the course.

Transcript.   A total record of classes taken, awards or credits granted to you, and your grades, throughout your college career. If you transfer schools, your transcript will be required by the Registrar at your new school.

Work-study program.   Jobs on campus that are available to students who meet the requirements for financial aid.

Skills to Master

There are a number of skills you can master that will help you get started off on the right foot.

   Establish a "things to do" list for the week. Always add new items as needed and check off what's been completed. You will feel a great sense of accomplishment as you start marking off the tasks that have been done. But be flexible. Change your schedule as often as necessary as new issues crop up, so that your agenda really works for you.

   Establish a comfortable place that you designate as your study area. Aim for spots that are well lit, free of distractions, and convenient for you. It won't make sense to consider a study hall in the library if it takes you 20 minutes to get there and you only have 45 minutes allotted to review your notes on a particular day. Whether it's a quiet lounge, a spot in the library, or your dorm room, establish it as a space where you can settle in and get to work. Let friends and roommates know that it's important that your study time is not interrupted. Keep all your needed equipment there, such as your calendar, pens, ruler, or calculator. It might even be the same space where you handle social and financial arrangements, so find a place for your date-book, your checkbook, bills, stamps, a telephone directory, and so on. Try not to let it get too cluttered as you will need your work and study areas to be available and ready for you to settle in at any time.

   Don't be a tough taskmaster. Give yourself a chance to stretch and take breaks as needed. Then return to your work without getting lured into conversations and lengthy telephone calls.

Note Taking

If you are not tape recording or relying on a note-taker, whatever notes you *do* take on your own are important. You become an active learner as you process information in your own words. Sit in the front of the room in order to avoid being distracted by others. Keep your attention focused on the lecturer. If you cannot write quickly, don't expect to get every word down. Try to develop your own style of shorthand so at least key words and main ideas get jotted down. Leave lots of space and wide margins on each page. You can always go back to fill in notes after the class or after conferring with other classmates.

Copy notes over if it helps you with memorization. Use colored highlighters to mark the main points and make important notes stand out. Reading your notes out loud may help you remember the material, too. And invent strategies that will help you recall what you need to know:

- Alphabetize
- Make rhymes
- Keep lists
- Think of associations to key words

Remember to copy whatever material the instructor writes on the board and what is frequently emphasized in the lecture. Chances are those are items or points you should be familiar with. Review your notes as soon as you can after each lecture. If you plan to tape record class lectures and discussions, be sure you label the cassettes before class, for example, "Intro. to Sociology, Sept. 20th, side I." Listen to tapes as soon as possible after each taping session.

Study Groups

If no organized study group exists, ask a classmate to join you for a snack while you review notes and go over material before an exam. You can ask each other questions and talk about the main issues covered in class lectures and reading assignments. You can ask the professor to help establish study groups for you, or at least make an announcement in the class so that other interested students can contact you.

Study Cards

You can make your own study cards to get organized for an exam. Ordinary 3" × 5" or 4" × 6" index cards are fine. Just list questions or problems on one side of the cards and a brief answer on the other side. Use your own words and try to include a key phrase or main issue to jog your memory as you review each card. Using flash cards like this really works well when you have a study partner.

Summarizing

This is a form of note-taking that helps organize information you need to learn. A summary will enable you to see the broad overview of a topic, rather than get caught up in a variety of smaller details. Identifying the main idea of a lecture or a reading assignment will provide you with a mini-version of the original material. This is merely additional practice for you to restate information in your own words to reinforce the learning.

Make a Date

You are expected to let the instructor know if you have questions or are unclear about topics covered in the class. It's up to you to make an appointment during his or her office hours. Go directly to the department secretary to arrange for this if the instructor doesn't have a sign-up sheet posted on the office door.

Written Assignments

Some of your written assignments may be more difficult and involved than the exams for a course. You need to fully understand the course and research material, not just memorize information. As you know, just guessing on an exam allows you to get the correct answer from time to time. There's really no room for guessing or fudging on research projects or reports. You are generally given ample time to prepare for the assignment. You can even discuss your paper with your tutor or see if your professor is willing to talk with you about it during office hours.

Think about these steps to get you started on your written projects:

- Think about the assignment. What are the specific requirements for length and format? Can you choose your own topic?
- Thoughtfully select a topic. Choose one of some interest to you.
- Utilize the library's resources, including the librarians.
- Read the necessary books, articles, and journals.
- Take notes on your research.
- Brainstorm on ideas that relate to the topic and use the best ideas as part of your outline.
- Organize all your data in an outline.
- Keep the main ideas and the supporting ideas in a logical sequence.
- Develop each idea as fully as you can and begin to organize your paragraphs.
- If required, take notes for a bibliography or for footnotes.
- Write one or more rough drafts.
- Edit the drafts.
- Write the final draft and put it into the format you've selected.
- Proofread the finished product.
- Pay attention to grammar, spelling, and punctuation.
- Don't forget about computers and spellchecks, and have another pair of eyes review your finished work.

An overwhelming project can always be broken down into much more manageable steps, such as the ones described here. Each step requires time set aside to handle it, and all the steps cannot be taken the day the project is due!

Test Taking

More than most other tasks, taking a test generates great anxiety for most students. With advance preparation you will have less anxiety and better performance. Although it's difficult, try to relax during exams. Be sure you arrange in advance whatever accommodations you require, such as a quiet room, a reader, or a scribe.

Scan the test first, so that you can plan your time and try to answer those questions that you find easier. Take time to read the exam directions carefully. If necessary, underline or circle what you are being asked to do. Tests often ask you to:

- Summarize
- Compare
- List
- Analyze

Follow the directions carefully. Begin by answering the questions that you feel are the easiest. Check or mark the more difficult ones, and return to them when you finish with the easier items.

If you don't fully understand a test question, let the proctor know. You can try to paraphrase it back to the proctor by restating it in your own words to be sure you truly understand what is being asked. Learn from each test experience what you can do better for the next exam. Go over your test performance with a counselor or with the instructor to analyze what may have gone wrong. You can then avoid that problem in the future.

Be Upbeat

You may need to psych yourself up each day to do your job—the job of being a student. This is particularly important when you're feeling anxious and stressed by the demands of college life. Focus on your past successes and on what you *can* do, not on your limitations. Make a connection on campus. We all need support from someone. Find one person on the campus who will listen to you as well as encourage you. Advisor, classmate, roommate, or office secretary—any empathic person you can link up with is fine.

Look for ways to do things better. Continue to get advice and assistance from the experts and those people on campus who care about your progress.

What You Can Do to Stay on Top

- Make sure your calendar is marked and up to date with projects and assignments that are due.

- Review your calendar at the start of every day.

- Once a week, organize your notes, files, appointment book, bills, and so on.

- Take notes and condense them into a summary of key ideas.

- Review all notes and handouts from lectures and readings.

- Read your notes aloud, and rewrite those notes if that helps you learn.

- Make study cards, outlines, charts, graphs, summaries—whatever works best for you.

- When reading, use a highlighter for points you want to remember.

- Keep a list of hard to understand concepts and discuss these with the instructor at the next class meeting.

- When studying for an exam, use all your materials: tapes, notes, handouts, summaries.

- Arrange to study with a partner or organize a small study group.

- It's okay to overlearn. Don't stop when you feel you know enough to pass the test. Allow your body of knowledge on the topic to grow as you immerse yourself in a subject and really explore it. This will make more sense than just memorizing random facts.

- Attend every class. You cannot afford to miss new material, or even material that is being reviewed.

- Always take full advantage of the resources and supports on the campus. Do this early in the semester. Don't wait until you are desperate for help.

- Be a self-advocate. Ask for help when you need it to keep you on track.

- Avoid making excuses—get beyond the "have pity on me" stage.

- Remember your health. You are now in charge of maintaining it. This includes a sensible diet, exercise, and rest.

- Surround yourself with people who see the positive side of situations. Negative behavior and attitudes destroy everyone's spirits.

- Observe others and learn what you can from those around you. Friends can help you learn about yourself and the world around you. Take a good look at the behavior of those you admire.

- Take responsibility. Don't transfer blame to a tough professor or an insensitive roommate. *You* are responsible for your own actions.

- Avoid old mistakes, but don't convince yourself that you are a failure if things don't work out exactly as planned. Acknowledge that you may have goofed and think about what you need to do to avoid repeating the mistake. You can learn to do a better job the next time.

- Learn to use a personal computer. Regardless of what your program is, a computer will be invaluable. Become familiar with word processing, database programs, and spreadsheets. It will help in college and be important on a job in the future.

- Learn how you learn best and stick with what works for you.

- Read bulletin boards around the campus, the school paper, and the local newspaper. This will allow you to stay on top of events and activities that may be of interest to you and enrich your academic and your social life.

- Don't give up. It may take several tries to reach your goal. Hang in and stay with what is important to you. It may make the difference between success and defeat.

- Go to class, go to class, go to class!

Treat college like a job. You'll reap the rewards of the effort you put into your college experience. **You are building a foundation for your future.**

Using Your College's Resources

Your College Library

Make the library one of the first areas you explore as you settle into campus life. Your college library will serve as an information center for:

- Books
- Audio and visual tapes
- Periodicals and reference works
- Guidebooks and directories
- Computer software
- Other materials in both print and electronic formats

You will probably be able to "talk" with other college or university libraries and even have use of their acquisitions, via a computer terminal in the library itself or in your dorm or study center. College libraries now use very sophisticated electronic indexes to access articles and texts.

Librarians and assistants in the research section are helpful people to know and work with. Sign up for a library tour if it is available. If not, you might want to make a point of meeting the librarian to help you get started. This is the place where you will probably research many of your term papers and other assignments. Many college libraries are divided into various sections.

Circulating books.   Books you can take out and return when they are due.

Reference collections.   Encyclopedias, dictionaries, and more.

Periodicals.   Daily, weekly, monthly, and annual newspapers and magazines, journals, and other similar publications.

Special collections.   Rare books and manuscripts, specialized materials, and government publications.

Reserve section.   Items placed "on hold" by faculty members for you to borrow for a limited time or use within the library.

"Where do you go for information for all of your class papers? How can you focus your search? Do you need generalized or specific information? How current is the information in your textbook? You may not realize that your college library is a good starting point to begin your search for information on *any* topic for *any* class and a great source of untapped information that will have answers to all of your questions. *Don't go through your college years avoiding the library*!
* Learn how to be an informed citizen.
* Learn how to use information in problem solving.
* Learn how to sift through information for effective decision making.
* Learn how to learn—*in the library*!"

Dr. Rochelle Sager
Director of Library and Media Services

Your College's Career Counseling and Placement Office

Career counseling is a critical part of your educational process of preparing you for your adult life as a productive member of the labor force. Your school's Career Counseling and Placement office is your connection between college and the world of work. Today's complex job market requires that you be more aware than ever of:

* Your own strengths and shortcomings

* Career information

Finding satisfaction and success in a career requires *planning* a career. A **career** is actually a broad concept that describes the kind of work you do. The most satisfied workers tend to be those whose jobs are a part of their career plan, rather than those who just "fall into" a job. Unlike the artist or writer who drives a taxicab to be able to pay the rent, a lab technician will probably feel more fulfilled when he or she has a job in the field of medicine.

How the Career Planning Process Works

- You will need to identify your values to get a clear picture of what you want in a career.

- You will need to identify and acknowledge both your strengths and your weaker areas.

- You will want to match this information to the most appropriate careers that you have researched.

- You will need to learn job search skills, such as how to get information, networking techniques, strategies for successful interviewing, putting together professional cover letters and résumés, or preparing a portfolio.

Career success is a lifelong journey. Begin thinking and planning yours as early as you can. Take full advantage of the many services that may be open to you. Far too often college students wait until their senior year to discover the professional services that are available as soon as you enter college. Begin early and **use all resources** that you need to plan your career and learn to be an effective job seeker. Career planning resources might include:

- Individual or group sessions with a career counselor

- Computerized career planning programs

- Career or vocational library

- Job referral services

- Seminars and panels with industry representatives or past graduates employed in various fields of work

- Workshops focusing on job search skills

- On-campus recruitment

- Industry mentor programs

- Co-op or internship programs

Once you have settled into college life, make an appointment with a career counselor to begin your career exploration. You will then begin to assess your values, interests, and skills. Your campus may have a SIGI, DISCOVER, or other computerized career planning program. Attend programs such as Career Fairs and Workshops, or campus appearances by industry representatives and college alumni speaking about their organizations and their jobs and career paths. Look into summer or part-time job possibilities as a means of investigating those industries you may want to consider.

Review your academic plans and incorporate skills courses that may be important to you in the fields you are considering. Build a strong relationship with your career counselor. It should be an ongoing one. In your second and third year, you might be ready to think about co-op or part-time positions. Prepare a resume and cover letter, with the help of the Career Services Office, for any interviews you arrange. Begin to research firms that may be on your On-Campus Recruitment list for your senior year.

In your last year, you'll want to take advantage of all workshops related to your industry of choice and your job hunt, and continue attending Career Days and Nights. Be sure to find out as much as you can about On-Campus Recruitment and the firms that participate in it. Check out those employers who offer summertime or apprenticeship programs for junior year students. This is an excellent way to get an early view of an organization and have them get to know you. It could pave the way to a more permanent work relationship.

On-Campus Recruitment

The employers who are part of your school's On-Campus Recruitment (OCR) program are specifically interested in meeting with soon-to-be graduates, who may be candidates for their firm's jobs or training programs. Don't miss the chance to learn which firms will visit your college campus and what positions they will be eager to fill. Your career counselor will be able to give you information about the OCR program.

Each campus has their own sign-up system for OCR interviews. You will need to work closely with your career counselor and be responsible for knowing each recruiter's arrangements, so that you don't miss out on meeting companies of real interest to you. In some cases, firms are happy to meet with all interested students and have an **open interview schedule**. Popular firms often find that they must limit the number of applicants on their interviewing schedule and have a **closed interview**

schedule. Before their campus visit, they review résumés of interested applicants and select those that are of greatest appeal to them. Or they might give your OCR coordinator a list of specific requirements and ask the coordinator to sort out those students who meet their standards and include them on their closed schedule. The list of requirements might include:

- A specific G.P.A.
- Certain technical or major courses taken and passed
- Particular skills, such as a foreign language or computer expertise
- Past summer or part-time work experience in the field
- Ability to relocate or travel extensively, if hired
- Driver's license

Summary: Preparing for the Future

- Make an appointment to meet with a career counselor as early as possible.
- Check out the availability of computerized career guidance systems. They're fun to use and can be very helpful.
- Attend career-related programs and workshops.
- Join clubs or groups on campus that reflect your career interest.
- Talk to professors in the courses that relate to your career goals. They can be a source of contacts and current labor market information.
- Use the school's vocational/career library to research career options.
- Look for part-time, summer, or volunteer jobs to explore various fields.
- Meet with alumni or industry mentors to conduct informational interviews about careers.
- Take advantage of any sessions focusing on career planning and job search skills, such as:

- Résumé and cover-letter writing
- Interview preparation
- Labor market information
- Research skills

- Find out about student chapters of professional organizations and societies.
- Explore internships and co-op opportunities in the career field of your choice.
- Keep in touch with your career counselor regularly to give updates on your employment status and discuss current job openings.

Give back generously. Once employed, don't forget to take the time to work with students doing the very things you attempted to do. Volunteer to participate in panel discussions and workshops. Become a mentor for students, and work with them as they explore their own career goals.

14

Time Management, Setting Goals, and Making Decisions

You can't stop the clock, but you *can* attempt to be in charge of it by understanding how to plan your priorities and how to **control the clock**. Managing time wisely is every person's challenge, and certainly affects every college student. Those with learning disabilities often lose track of time. Thus you need to acquire solid time management skills.

Making Time Work Best for You

A good deal of your time will be spent *away* from the classroom. Learning to use that time wisely will be a key to your survival in college. To begin to use your time more effectively, there are a number of issues you need to think about.

Know Your Highs and Lows

Do you really come alive at night, or do you shine early in the morning or in the middle of the day? If you know your peak energy periods and your low energy times, you can use that information to help you plan your schedule. A "morning person" is wise to get up an hour or so earlier a couple of times a week to study or have a review session. Plan the tough or important tasks around your high energy period, those times when you feel fresh and alert. Use lower energy times for less intense, less important activities. Body temperature and our own body's daily rhythm actually determine the times of the day that we feel sleepy or more alert. A morning person's body temperature rises one or two degrees, usually at 8 or 9 in the evening, causing a feeling of sleepiness. A night person's temperature doesn't rise until 1 or 2 in the morning.

Know Your Attention Limits

You need to know how much time you should plan for library research, study sessions, or homework assignments—based on your *own* capacity to stay focused and on task. Your involvement in any project should stop *before* you start to feel restless and distracted.

Know Your Preferences

Are you more at home with a daily routine that is fairly consistent? Do you feel more comfortable knowing what to expect each day? Or would you rather have a less predictable schedule, one that includes a bit more variety? Doing some of the same things every day establishes a rhythm that some people find helpful. Others find routines boring. Think about how detailed you want your daily "things to do" list to be. Some students prefer to complete a given task at a single sitting and get it over with, while others need to break tasks down into smaller segments and tackle one small step at a time. Plan for whichever option suits you best.

Know What the Consequences May Be

Carefully consider the various options you may have. Only you can make the critical decision of whether to tackle the week-old pile of laundry or use the time to do library research. Think through the consequences of each decision to determine which choice is really more important and what the consequence of not handling either choice might be.

Know What Is Realistic for You

Be sensible about how much time you should allow for your chores and assignments. Add more time than you think you'll need for the really important projects. One crisis or another usually has a way of arising and you'll handle it with much more ease if you don't have to deal with added time pressures.

Know What's Necessary

Certain activities just cannot be avoided, such as meetings, scheduled events, banking chores, paying bills, and time spent in traveling, calling, writing home, and so on. These are obligations that you probably *have* to fulfill, so accept them and attempt to handle them efficiently. If telephone calls start to become unmanageable, however, keep a clock or a timer right next to your phone and end your call tactfully after three or five minutes.

Know How to Combine Simple Tasks

You might be able to review your calendar for the next day while you are having a bedtime snack, or use breakfast time to go over your daily list of "things to do." Why not review the day's mail during lunch or use the time you spend chatting on the phone to polish your shoes or iron your clothes?

Know How to Organize

Invest in a batch of highlighters and folders (or large envelopes, small bins, trays, or baskets) to keep your various notes and papers together in an organized way. Begin to color-code papers and materials you need to file so that everything for a particular course is easy to identify.

Devise categories that make sense for your needs, put everything into the relevant folder. The categories might include:

- Each course you are taking
- Club or extracurricular activities
- Invitations
- Bills to be paid
- Doctor or dental appointments
- Conferences with professors, counselors, and advisors
- Receipts
- Anything else you need to file and save

Managing Time—How Well Do You Do?

Complete this list of questions to give yourself a picture of how well you currently use your time. Circle either Yes or No in the columns on the right.

1. Do you use a calendar to note important events, projects, and due dates?	Yes	No
2. Do you set daily priorities for how you will use your time?	Yes	No
3. Do you stick to your priority list?	Yes	No
4. Do you try to get to the most important or most difficult tasks first?	Yes	No
5. Do you make every effort to complete what you start?	Yes	No
6. Do you plan ahead for long-term assignments?	Yes	No
7. Do you plan small, manageable steps to break down a large project?	Yes	No
8. Do you avoid being sidetracked just when you're ready to study?	Yes	No
9. Do you set realistic time frames for your studying and stick to them?	Yes	No
10. Do you say "no" when you are *really* burdened and cannot handle more socializing?	Yes	No

If you've said "Yes" to the majority of these questions, you are aware of how effective you can be when you plan for your use of time. If you have an overload of "no" responses, you need to learn more about time management strategies and put them into practice.

Summary: Managing Your Time

- Always keep a calendar, a date book, and a simple list of things that you need to do daily.

- Prioritize your tasks daily, based on what needs to be done first.

- Check off your chores as you finish them. It's important for you to see what you have accomplished.

- Make time for everything that is important to you. Be realistic about what you can accomplish in a given time frame.

- Finish the critical tasks.

- Eliminate or delegate less pressing chores. Not all tasks are equally important.

- Be flexible with your time schedule—changes *will* be necessary at times.

- Work on high-level concentration activities during your peak energy times.

- Deal with big or difficult projects by breaking them down into smaller achievable steps.

- Learn to say "no" when it is appropriate, so that you don't jeopardize your personal, school, or leisure time.

- Always plan for the predictable, routine chores, and leave time for the unexpected.

- Don't strive for perfection in every task. Complete them well enough to get the results that you need.

- Be sure you allow time to relax and re-charge. Plan for this down time as well as for work and study time.

- Reward yourself for a job well done or a goal that you've met.

Setting Goals

Some of us are able to achieve whatever we set our sights on, with ease. The rest of us seem to stumble along the way or fall far from our goal. If you are determined to master the technique of setting and reaching your goals, realize that the basic rules of setting goals are relatively simple.

Your first step is to identify *what* it is that you want to achieve, to change, or to master. If you only have a vague idea in mind, you are not quite ready to move ahead. But half-formed wishes do develop into definite and clear commitments. Once you have a concrete goal in mind, you will be able to move ahead.

Identify What Needs to Be Done and Write It Down

Be clear about what you are aiming for and make a serious commitment to achieving it. You can break down what appears to be an overwhelming step into a series of less intimidating actions. Let's say that your goal is to get into a college. If this seems too scary to tackle, and fear prevents you from getting started from taking any action at all, here's how you might break down some of the activities you need to handle:

- Begin by writing or calling for school catalogs.
- Use the library or purchase several manuals and how-to guides about tackling college entrance procedures—just as you're doing right now!
- Talk to college students and graduates that you know who might have some advice or suggestions for you.
- Go to a local college and arrange for an appointment with an admissions counselor.
- Start compiling a file of information you will need once you begin to send out applications and admissions forms.

Simply taking any one of these small steps will give you the confidence and momentum to go on to the next step. You can also make a list of what you need to do and what information you still need to find out, and move on to tackling that.

Set a Time Limit

Don't allow the sense of an endless amount of time to hamper you from forging ahead. But *do* stay flexible. If your goal is to gather college catalogs in six weeks so that you can begin to review them, don't consider this step a failure if they haven't all arrived by the sixth week. Certain things (such as the mail service) are out of your control. You have reached your goal when you have received and reviewed all the catalogs you were interested in.

Develop a Plan of Action

If you are well organized, you can establish a plan of action and set a date for each step you will take. You can also decide what you will ask others to do for you.

Get Help Where You Can

Share your goal with people who can help you move things along. A student at a college that interests you might bring home a copy of the school catalog on the next vacation break so you can avoid waiting for it in the mail. The student may even be able to chat with you about personal experiences with the admissions interview or about entrance requirements.

Be Flexible

You need to be determined and committed to reaching your goal, but don't be stubborn and rigid. Situations and conditions are apt to change. Adjust your plans and your timetable to reflect what is realistic as you attempt to move closer and closer to your target.

Be Expansive

Review your lists of goals and action plans frequently. It's fine to have several plans operating if you can juggle more than one at a time. You can be finishing high school, gathering college admissions information and hunting for a summer job—all at the same time!

Summary: Setting and Reaching Your Goals

- Identify your goal
- Write it down
- Set a reasonable time limit
- Develop a plan of action
- Get the help that you need
- Be flexible
- Be expansive

Making Decisions

You make decisions—both simple and very complicated ones—every single day. Whether you are solving a problem or deciding on which course of action to take, you are making decisions that will affect every area of your life. You make hundreds of daily decisions so quickly and effortlessly that you tend not to pay much attention to them. You may not even think of them as decisions. Consider this: When you got out of bed this morning you made more than a dozen different decisions:

- What time to get out of bed
- Whether to hop out of bed or get up slowly
- Whether to shower or not to shower
- Whether to shampoo your hair today
- Whether or not to brush your teeth before breakfast
- Which toothpaste to use
- Whether to get breakfast started or to skip it today

As the stakes get higher and the risks increase, many people are unable to make any decision or move in any direction without great discomfort and anxiety. For simple decisions, chances are you just follow your usual routine and don't consider a step-by-step approach to making decisions. But when faced with a major decision, you will want to think carefully, consider the alternatives, and study the consequences.

Making a decision often feels tough because it involves taking a risk. If the risk is high, and the outcome of the decision is important, your anxiety level is sure to rise. No matter how much advice and input your friends, family, or counselors give you, the decision is ultimately yours.

Most of us end up with some degree of anxiety in the decision-making process. The greater the anxiety, the more time and thought is generally needed to make the decision.

Some prefer to rely on others—their parents or siblings, a best friend or a trusted teacher—to take the burden of this responsibility out of their control. Others feel they have no control at all over their life and adopt a "whatever will be, will be" point of view. There is really no such thing as *not* making a decision. All that means is that you have decided to do *nothing*. And *no* decision is certainly a choice in itself. Many of us tend to put off making effective choices by coming up with excuses such as:

- I'll deal with it tomorrow, next week, or next month...

- I can't make up my mind right now.

- Whatever happens, happens!

- This choice I'm making just "feels right."

- If it's okay with you, I guess it's okay with me.

We are often anxious because making a decision can also mean making a change. Many people fear making a decision of any importance because they think it will be irreversible and will shape their lives forever. But chances are the decisions you make will not be *permanent* and can be changed at some point. You may feel uncomfortable selecting from among a few choices, but the toughest decisions are really those that present us with many options and an open-ended deadline. More choices certainly increase our sense of freedom, but they can also bring on a sense of confusion. If too many options lead to stalling, our procrastination will force a decision to be made for us by default. *Procrastination is a pitfall*!

We all differ in so many ways, including how we make decisions, whether they are trivial or critical ones. We might:

- Do anything that is suggested just to get it over with ....
  (IMPULSIVE)

- Leave the choice to chance by flipping a coin ....(FATALISTIC)

- Depend on our intuition by relying on how we feel about
  the issue ....(INTUITIVE)

- Put the decision off and do nothing...(PROCRASTINATION)

A tough decision, such as what college to attend or what course of study or program to select, will probable require more thought and attention than more routine decisions. Using a logical decision-making process will help you make better and more effective decisions. A step-by-step decision-making process might allow you to make choices that really work for you. Such a process may help you to:

- Identify the decision you need to make
- Gather the information you need
- Identify the choices available to you
- Select the best choices
- Choose one option
- Take some action
- Evaluate the results of that action

This relatively simple decision-making process may help you take control of your decisions—and find them more satisfying! Remember: When you are faced with a major decision, it *can* be broken down into smaller ones. Your plan should be to break big decisions down into smaller parts and then deal with the manageable parts. Once you tackle the smaller parts, you are closer to solving the big problem.

Get Ready to Decide: Taking It Step by Step

You need to get ready to make *any* decision. Make preparations for your decision by reviewing some questions.

- Is your goal clear to you?
- Are you clear about exactly what needs to be decided upon and resolved?
- Are you the only person who will make the decision? If someone else is involved or will be affected, involve that person from the start of the decision-making process.
- What is the timetable? You need to know *when* this decision must be made. What time limits exist?
- Do you have all the information that you need? Have you done all the necessary research and fact-finding?
- What are the risks involved? Are you willing to accept the risks? If not, you need to discard that option.
- Are you ready to take action? Do you have the time, money, equipment, people, or whatever else it will take to act on your decision?

Once you have thought about and answered these questions, you are most likely ready to move on to the decision-making step.

Conflict in Decision Making

Every time a decision needs to be made or a problem needs to be solved, you face some conflict. You may have to choose between two things you would like to do or perhaps you'll need to select the lesser of "two evils." Sometimes you will face an alternative that has both positive and negative aspects attached to it.

Identify your needs

Frequently, the hardest part of the decision-making process is simply figuring out what you really want in the way of a solution. To begin, make a list for yourself of the things you'd like to result from a particular decision. Let's say the issue is about what major you should choose in college. You might list all of the pros and cons of the two or three fields of study that appeal to you. Research the fields to determine what starting salaries might be upon graduation, what typical career paths are like, how available work is for a beginner, and so on. It's possible that with the major you choose you would have to relocate to get entry-level work. If that is out of the question for you—or at least a last choice—you might have to look at other fields that do not require relocation for employment.

Once you have the pros and cons down on paper, it will be easier for you to rank your preferences by sorting out what is absolutely essential in a career path for you, and what is really of little importance to you. This will help you establish a concrete sense of where you stand on the issue.

Expand your choices

It's always in your best interest to increase the number of options open to you. Sometimes just a casual conversation with friends, family, or classmates will suggest alternatives for you to consider. Chances are, the more choices you have available to you, the more satisfying your ultimate decision will be. It often helps to try to look at the situation differently and open your eyes to other options. Learn to be a good gatherer of information. Talk to your friends, roommates, counselors, and librarians. Get all the data you need so that you can be comfortable about your final choice.

Approach the problem from a different angle

If you can "step outside of yourself" and just imagine you are someone else reviewing the situation you are grappling with, you might have a different take on the problem. Exploring other points of view can help you get "unstuck." You can even pretend that you are your own friend and just give the kind of advice you'd ordinarily give to a friend in a similar situation. It can sometimes be easier to recognize solutions or ideas for others that you can't see when you are too caught up in the dilemma.

Another way to develop additional options might be through **brainstorming**. Brainstorming is merely the technique of gathering *all* ideas and possible solutions without rejecting *anything*. The fast flow of uncensored ideas often triggers creative thinking and allows one idea to lead to others. When doing this with one or more friends, it should be fast-paced and without interruption to generate the best of your thinking. There's always time to judge and rule out ideas that are unworkable *after* the brainstorming session is over. Someone needs to keep a written list of everything that is mentioned, or you can use a tape recorder.

Risk taking

Understanding your own tolerance for risk may help lessen your fears about making decisions. Here are several choices to think about.

- You can choose the safest option—avoiding all high-risk choices.

- You can play the odds wisely—choosing the option with the greatest chance of success.

- You could go for broke—going with the choice that has the outcome you really want, *regardless of the consequences*. Do this only if you are *sure* that you can live with the outcomes, or if you won't be happy unless you give it a try.

How Ready Are You to Make Sound Decisions?

Circle either True or False, according to what makes sense for you.

1. I don't bother making decisions, as I have no control over my life.   True   False

2. I usually make a decision if something feels right to me.   True   False

3. The best decisions I make are when I have all the facts I need.   True   False

4. I often feel that there are only one or two choices in issues.   True   False

5. I really try to get as much information as possible before I make a decision.   True   False

6. I like to think about how my decision will affect me or anyone else involved.   True   False

7. I don't even bother to think about the consequences of my decisions.   True   False

8. Even if I avoid making a decision, things
   seem to work out well for me.   True   False

9. I like to know what my friends want me to
   do before I make my decision.   True   False

10. I like to get input from concerned others
    before I make my decisions.   True   False

11. I consider all of my options before I decide.   True   False

12. Decisions are easy for me to make—it's
    either one choice or the other.   True   False

If you circled True for numbers 3, 5, 6, 10, and 11, and False for the rest, you have a good idea of your ability to take charge of the decision-making process. You have a choice between making an *active* decision and a *passive* decision...between taking charge of your life or feeling as if life is taking charge of you.

Here's an exercise that will give you a chance to practice some decision-making techniques and show you that it is possible to develop additional alternatives when you are struggling with a decision.

A. Describe a decision you are currently involved in making.

_____

_____

B. Jot down the options you see open to you.

_____

_____

_____

C. Try to brainstorm with friends or family to expand those options. Be sure to list everything without discussing or eliminating what is offered.

_____

_____

_____

_____

D. Be your own best friend and try to think of the kind of advice you'd offer to another person in this situation. Write it down.

_____

_____

E. Review and compare all your new solutions to come up with the best possible choices.

_____

_____

_____

Summary: Effective Decision Making

You will probably feel better if you *know* as well as *feel* that you are making the best choice at the time. Use the simple decision-making steps. Your most effective decision making will happen with a thoughtful and planned approach.

- Identify the problem, question, or conflict you need to re-solve.

- List realistic options. Avoid those options that include un-acceptable risks.

- Gather information about likely outcomes of the options and how it might affect you or others.

- Assess the risks.

- Decide which option gives you the best possible outcome.

- Develop a back-up plan in case it is needed.

- Take action.

- Evaluate how well your choice is working for you.

- Be flexible. Your needs may change as you learn more about the consequences of decisions.

- Try to relax. Almost every decision can be changed.

Feel positive about your decision-making skills. You have the ability to make choices and decisions wisely!

15

Choosing a Career

Wouldn't it be great to:

- Wake up and go to work with a positive attitude?
- Enjoy most of the duties that are a part of your job?
- Use the skills and talents you are most proud of?
- Feel that there's room for you to learn and grow?
- Feel comfortable with your boss and your co-workers?
- Know that you can handle your job responsibilities?
- Feel good about yourself at the end of a workday?

For some people, most of the items listed are a reality of their work life! Yet for countless others, work represents a series of jobs that are dull, unrewarding, and offer no challenge.

Work is one of the most central activities in our lives. It often defines who we are by:

- Using our talents and skills
- Financially supporting our lifestyle
- Allowing us to take pride in our accomplishments
- Giving us the opportunity to contribute to our community or to society

Choice Instead of Chance

For many students, education can lead them in the direction of a satisfying career path. Whether you test the waters of the work world upon graduation, or you decide to explore career paths while still in school, it's essential to think about and to clarify your career goals as early as possible. **Your educational planning can then take your career goals into account**. Your career choice is a critical one. Your future success and happiness lies with your discovery of what satisfies you most. College is the perfect place for this sort of self-assessment. Also, find time to:

- Take an internship, part-time job, or work as a volunteer
- Get involved with student government or clubs on campus, to gain leadership and teamwork experience
- Become computer literate or upgrade your existing computer skills

In the past college students prepared for careers that would last them a lifetime. Even in the 1980s, most beginning workers believed that if they found an entry job they liked, they could look forward to career growth and years of job security. In today's competitive marketplace, that is no longer the case. The workplace of the 21st century will be very challenging, and the major changes that began in the 1990s will continue to affect businesses all across America. Your role as a worker, particularly as a new worker, will be more demanding than ever.

To lower the cost of doing business, many firms are reducing the size of their workforce. Called "downsizing," this change forces new employees to quickly master basic skills and show how productive and effective they can be. Many leaner companies with fewer managers are now expecting **teams of workers** to collaborate, plan, and assist in projects. Entry-level workers who work well in a team setting, and thrive with less management direction and more peer interaction, will be at a definite advantage.

These days, college students need to consider multiple choices and changes. You'll need to have plans that are flexible and be aware of the occupational forecasts for the 21st century. Our manufacturing economy is quickly shifting to a service-based economy, which calls for professional, managerial, and technically skilled workers.

Experts predict that by the year 2000, large numbers of jobs will be found in the service occupations, such as the collecting, analyzing, storing, and retrieval of information. Hot career choices for the 21st century might fall into these categories:

- Accounting
- Computers
- Health care
- Hospitality and travel

It is predicted that the real job growth will be in small to mid-sized firms, while larger organizations attempt to pare down for more efficient operation. The critical career choice you'll need to make may be a process that you'll repeat several times in your work life.

Career Exploration

Making a career choice is a major decision. National surveys tell us that over 70 percent of American workers are not happy with their jobs. Don't become a part of that gloomy statistic. To determine what career is right for you, you need to have adequate and accurate vocational information. You need to learn how to research career information and relate what you learn to your own personal characteristics and desired lifestyle. If you remain in the dark about available career opportunities or options, your career-related decisions may not be very fulfilling.

- Self-awareness is a critical first step in making a vocational decision.
- Effective career decisions allow you to realize your individual interests, needs, and values.
- Your career choice affects your *total* lifestyle.

Learn about yourself

Identify your:

- Skills

- Interests
- Values
- Personal qualities

Learn about the work world

- Research jobs and career paths
- Explore career fields
- Determine career goals and immediate job objectives

Learn about job hunting

Familiarize yourself with job search strategies such as:

- Networking
- Informational interviewing
- Interview techniques
- Cover-letter and resume writing
- Negotiating salaries
- Decision making

You can acquire the skills required to plan a career and conduct a job search. Once learned, those skills will be yours for a lifetime!

Finding Out What Works for You

Your first job in making your career decision is learning what you can about yourself, and then matching that information with your knowledge of various occupations and career paths. Once you are able to identify your own areas of strengths and weaknesses, you can select work areas that draw on your best skills. And you'll also be able to comfortably convey this important information to prospective employers when you begin your job hunt!

The process of career planning and exploration requires time and attention. It is a process that will eventually allow you to really understand much of what makes you tick—your interests, your abilities, your work-related values, and the special skills that you have or may decide to acquire.

Once you have this information under your belt, you can then examine areas of work that interest you and are a good fit with your particular attributes. We all know people who have known since grade school *exactly* what they want to be. For these lucky few, that's fine! But we also know that many adults are dissatisfied with the way they have spent years of their lives. They feel burdened by unsatisfying and unrewarding careers. Many middle-aged people still could not tell you the kind of work they feel they are best suited for, or even what jobs they might find most exciting and gratifying. Frequently, these people work in fields where jobs were available for them, rather than where they had an opportunity to select work that interested and challenged them. The decision was made by chance, not choice.

It is vital for all career planners to get an accurate picture of their strong points and just as important to acknowledge weaker areas to be able to avoid career mismatches. Moreover, responsibility for planning a career belongs to **you and you alone**. Your career counselor, friends, family, and professors can and should make suggestions and offer advice. But you must feel that *you* are in the driver's seat in making such an important decision. *You need to put together a picture of what is important to you, what you enjoy, what you are good at, and what your limitations are.*

Business is constantly changing. To get a job and grow in it requires anticipating what the next change may be and how you can remain valuable to your firm. Employers screen job applicants carefully to determine if they will add to the company's productivity. You will have to convince prospective employers and recruiters of your interest in learning and growing with their organization. It will be up to you to let others know how productive you can be as you compete for entry-level jobs. You can do this successfully once you have a clear view of exactly what you can offer and what you would like to develop further in yourself. You'll need to set your sights on a flexible job path and keep improving your knowledge and your skills. To do this, you need to be familiar with job search skills, such as:

- Job interviewing strategies
- Résumé and cover-letter writing

- Gathering occupational information
- Researching the labor market
- Preparing a portfolio if the field requires it

It will help you begin this ongoing career planning process if you are fairly familiar with your own particular learning style. This lifelong journey will always require some fine tuning every now and again, but you will be in charge of it once you master the career development areas described in this book.

You have the power to determine your future and *you* are the key force in doing so. Use that power to ensure your success by giving enough time and thought to planning your career. Then work to make your plan a reality!

It's Your Career: Take Charge of It!

Career satisfaction means different things to different workers. For some, it conjures up the idea of starting and growing a small business. You may want to experience life in the corporate world. Or you may decide to live the life of a freelancer, and use your special talents in a rural workshop away from the pressures of urban life. Or perhaps you are drawn to a career in city government, or want to be a part of a community agency that works with the elderly or the homeless. Define your own preferences and have back-up choices as well. Employment experts say we should all expect to have multiple careers as we enter the 21st century. A typical worker is going to have five or more different careers in a lifetime. That in itself is a good reason to develop a career plan and review it frequently so that it reflects your latest and your best thinking.

There are no guarantees in life, and you may not always find a job that's consistently challenging and financially rewarding. But you should expect the best you can get for yourself. Invest the time and effort needed to develop your own realistic profile.

All plans should be open to revision whenever it seems appropriate. That might mean as soon as next semester or in the far distant future. For all of us, career planning is an ongoing event, one that needs to be reviewed and revised as we grow and gain exposure to new and enriching experiences. Life in college may certainly change your thoughts about your future as a worker!

Your goal at this point is to increase your self-awareness and gather information about educational and career alternatives. Set aside time to investigate the Career Planning Office once you have settled into college life. Career counseling professionals will take you through the self-assessment and career exploration process. And now, most colleges have computerized career guidance systems. They are fun to operate, user-friendly, and will provide you with a wealth of information. You will want to:

Assess your own skills.   Become aware of the skills, aptitudes, and interests you possess, as well as areas you'd be willing to learn about or develop more fully to get you started on the career path of your choice.

Let yourself go.   Be expansive in your thinking and dreaming. Now is the time to explore every possibility. Unleash your imagination as you think about ways in which you'd like to be spending your work and leisure time.

Develop your career goals.   You will need to spend time discovering what is really important to you. Then you can more easily think about planning your future years as a member of the workforce. You'll gain insight into what you truly enjoy doing and what you do well, and start taking those first steps to make your dreams a reality.

Learn to market yourself.   Once you are clear about what you can offer a prospective employer, you will need those job search skills that help you present yourself in the most effective manner.

How to Begin

Your first step should be a visit to your college's Career Counseling or Career Planning Office. A professional career counselor will guide you through all stages of the career planning process. A great deal of the information you need to make a wise career choice will be available through the process of **self-assessment** or **self-exploration**.

Through self-assessment, you will identify your personal characteristics and important skills as well as take a look at your attitudes, values, interests, and work preferences. Only then can you begin to focus on exploring careers. In our rapidly changing society, it's not enough to explore just one occupation with the notion that once you are working in the field you are set for life. So you'll want to plan for this and become familiar with different occupations that match your own interests and skills, as well as your preferred style of living. This is a great start in preparing for your future.

Learning about Yourself

It's not easy for us to start really learning about ourselves, and it's even more difficult to share that information with others. It often takes a lifetime to understand what motivates and drives us. As we develop and change, our needs and interests change as well. You now need to start identifying your own job-related "needs." Begin to really view yourself as a *worker* and think about the tasks you may be doing for the next 40 years. Does that sound like a long time? That's often how long a person spends at work during a lifetime. Make your work an exciting adventure for yourself, by gathering as much information as you can about yourself and possible career choices.

It is indeed a process of discovery once you start identifying your own interests, skills, and abilities. Taking an inventory of what you like to do, what you do well, and what you want to do in the future is the first step in the self-assessment process. If you match your strong points with the skills required in certain careers, you will be able to blend your best qualities with an employer's requirements. This process also allows you to explore, as well as eliminate, career options before you settle on your final choices.

Your career counselor may encourage you to take a variety of self-directed inventories, which can provide information about your job activity preferences, personality type, interests, abilities, and values. There is no one ideal inventory or checklist that will answer all your questions and magically point you on a career path. But any of them may offer valuable clues about your ideas about work, and help you line them up with career options that make sense for you. Don't worry too much about which particular methods are used to get you thinking. The important thing is to get started in the career planning process.

Vocational Rehabilitation Services

Vocational rehabilitation, often referred to as **VR** or **Voc. Rehab.**, is a nationwide federal and state program that works with eligible people with disabilities to determine an employment goal and help them find employment. VR agencies can offer counseling and financial assistance. Training and education at a technical school or a college is often part of the plan. All states have a VR agency, with district offices located throughout the state. Your career counselor, librarian, or health care worker should be able to direct you. You will find a local listing in a telephone directory for your region, or by requesting a States Agency List from:

> The National Rehabilitation Information Center
> NARIC
> 8455 Colesville Road, Suite 935
> Silver Spring, MD 20910
> (800) 346-2742

If you go to a VR agency, you will be asked to fill out an application that asks for personal data that will determine your eligibility for service. You can get help in completing that application form in the VR office. You may be asked to supply your assigned counselor with school records, a work history, and medical information. If you need to have updated psychological or medical tests performed, it is likely that VR will cover those expenses. To be eligible for rehabilitation services, it must be determined that:

1. You have a physical or mental disability.
2. That disability causes a substantial handicap to employment.
3. There is reasonable expectation that vocational rehabilitation services will make you employable.

It may take some time before your eligibility is determined, so you need to be prepared for a wait in some cases. Of course, eligibility is determined without regard to race, sex, color, creed or national origin. VR may pay for all or a part of the services you need. If your income allows you to contribute toward those services, you will be asked to do so. You should apply for federal student financial aid, as VR agencies work directly with college financial aid officers to sort out what part of the school expenses will be handled by VR.

Once you are eligible, you and your counselor will work out an Individualized Written Rehabilitation Plan (IWRP). This plan clearly states the services that will be provided for you and your employment goals. Your VR counselor can be a valuable ally who will be helpful in assuring the smooth delivery of services and helpful in obtaining appropriate employment.

Self-Assessment

Self-assessment will help you determine:

- What you like to do
- What you do well
- The right work environment for you

Values

The first step in your search for career satisfaction should be defining what you actually like and dislike about work. These items are called your **work values**. Defining them will help you put together a clearer picture of what you might like in a career. Your values define you as a unique individual, though they are influenced by your family, friends, teachers, and culture.

It's helpful to identify those areas that are the most meaningful to you and then prioritize them. What matters to you about work-related issues may have little or no meaning to someone else. Some people put great emphasis on job security or a position of leadership, while others value a contribution to society or a prestigious title. Values are very personal. There are no "right" or "wrong" choices, only those that seem most appropriate for you. Try to sort out what is truly important to you, understanding that your list of values and how you rank them will change and grow as you do.

Career decisions are an expression of our needs and our values. Therefore, the ability to identify and clarify values is very important. A poorly defined value system can easily lead to career confusion, dissatisfaction, and frustration.

- Your values must be a reflection of your own choices.
- They must be prized by you, not imposed on you by others.

Use the list of typical values below to begin to build your *own* list of work values. Or start from scratch by thinking about and jotting down those areas of work that have importance for you. Make your list as long as you like, aiming for at least 10 to 12 items. Keep in mind that a satisfying choice is one that reflects your personal and work values. You need to be clear about items that are important to you, so that you won't be disappointed if you discover that certain career areas have standards or requirements that you are not comfortable with. In addition to prioritizing your values, examine those choices and decisions you've already committed yourself to. Why did you decide to go to college? To prepare for a career? To get away from home? To meet new friends? To learn new things? To satisfy the expectations of your family?

It's often difficult to separate our work-related values from those we value off the job. Check the ten items on the following list that you feel are the most important to you.

Next, eliminate the ten that are the least important to you.

Feel free to add any other items that are not listed. Then rank your top five values and cross off the five least important values on the list.

Can you now identify at least five values that you would not consider giving up?

_____ Urban location   _____ Wealth

_____ Economic security   _____ Lots of leisure time

_____ Creative work   _____ Work you enjoy

_____ Power   _____ Challenge

_____ Independence   _____ Prestige

_____ Ability to travel on the job

_____ Helping others

_____ Leadership role

_____ Having significant responsibilities

_____ Chance for growth and advancement

_____ Rural setting

_____ (add your own choices)

_____ _____

_____ _____

_____ _____

_____ Flexible hours

_____ Professional status

_____ Ability to work in a team setting

_____ No decision-making worries

_____ Tuition reimbursement

_____ Variety in job duties

_____ _____

_____ _____

_____ _____

_____ _____

Think about the following categories of work-related values, which may give you some ideas of what you would like to add to your list.

Social Impact

- Working for peace
- Helping the underprivileged and the homeless
- Improving race relations
- Conserving the environment

Work Conditions

- Friendly co-workers
- Modern environment
- Urban or rural setting
- Stress-free environment
- Non-traditional work hours
- Ability to work at home or in your own studio

Personal Preferences

- Risk taking
- Independence
- Creative environment
- Intellectually stimulating
- Frequent travel
- Work abroad
- Work in a team
- Work alone
- Prestige position
- Public service
- High-visibility position
- Impressive title

Your Own Role

- Work independently without much direction from a supervisor
- Chance for rapid advancement
- Able to follow specific directions
- Creative work
- Able to make decisions
- Training others
- Supervising others
- Able to be an entrepreneur
- Wide variety of job duties

Economic Benefits

- Generous vacation
- High salary
- Job security
- Good retirement and pension plan

- Strong benefits package for health and dental care

You may also want to think about the following:

- What kind of worker would you like to be ten years from now?

- Which of your family's values are the most important to you? Which values are less important to you?

- Who are two of your heroes or heroines? Why do you admire these people?

- Who are the most important people in your life?

- If you had the freedom to do anything at all that was related to work, what would you do?

- If you could spend any amount of money, exactly how would you spend it?

- If you had the luxury of learning about any field at all, with no time restrictions, what would you choose to learn?

- If you could have any job right now, what job would that be?

- Can you picture yourself in a "dream job"?
  - What would you be doing?
  - What skills would you use?
  - Would you work as part of a team, or alone?
  - Would you direct or supervise others?

Skills

Our skills often determine what career we choose. What have you enjoyed doing and what have you accomplished? It may have involved your strongest skills. Examine your accomplishments closely to see if they indicate a possible career direction for you, or if they confirm vocational choices you have already made. The task of identifying and recognizing your own talents and abilities is the next step. You want to be able to comfortably discuss with prospective employers your job-related skills. These skills are the heart of your résumé, yet most of us have a tough time describing the things we do best, whether we get paid for doing them or not.

What follows is a simple checklist of skills broken down into categories. Read each list and check those skills you feel you have. Don't be concerned at this point whether or not you enjoy using the skill. Just decide whether you can do it, and if so, check it off.

Clerical Skills

Working as part of a team
Working in an office
Following directions
Doing routine office work
Handling telephones
Data entry

Research Skills

Collecting data
Writing reports
Recognizing problems
Interviewing people
Developing questionnaires
Working without direction
Working on long-term projects

Communication Skills

Public speaking
Reading
Explaining and defining
Reasoning
Organizing
Writing

Manual Skills

Basic mechanics
Basic plumbing
Basic electronics
Precision machine work
Working on an assembly line
Working independently

Service Skills

Working under stress
Counseling
Guiding
Leading
Coordinating
Responding to emergencies
Working irregular hours

Public Relations

Working with people
Meeting deadlines
Informing the public
Planning
Maintaining a positive image
Researching
Writing news releases

Technical Skills

Evaluating data
Calculating
Following specifications
Adjusting controls
Drafting
Designing

Financial Skills

Calculating
Projecting
Budgeting
Handling detail work
Data processing
Accounting procedures
Strong concentration

Management Skills

Organizing
Planning
Directing
Scheduling
Delegating
Working with people
Training and supervising

Selling Skills	**Maintenance Skills**	**Agricultural Skills**
Contacting	Repairing equipment	Manual labor
Persuading	Maintaining equip-	Working outdoors
Reviewing products	ment	Operating basic ma-
or services	Operating machines	chinery
Informing buyers	Using tools	Repairing machinery
Promoting sales	Lifting heavy gear	Construction
Working with the	Working indoors or	Dealing with crops
public	outdoors	Dealing with ani-
Working irregular	Basic mechanical,	mals
hours	electrical, and	
	plumbing knowl-	
	edge	

List the categories where you had the most check marks. Your highest skills are:

1. _____

2. _____

3. _____

4. _____

5. _____

Interests

What do you like to do? What *don't* you like to do? An easy way to start identifying your interests is to simply scan this list and check the areas that have some appeal to you.

- Photography
- Outdoor work
- Art
- Consulting with others
- Changing systems
- Doing physical work
- Organizing

- Public speaking
- Architecture
- Biology
- Writing articles or stories
- Editing
- Publishing
- Building or constructing

- Health and medicine
- Analyzing data
- Selling
- Acting
- Operating machinery
- Teaching
- Using computers
- Crafts
- Traveling
- Military
- Gardening
- Cooking and entertaining
- Clerical work
- Repairing
- Working with animals
- Inventing
- Working with children
- Music
- Doing research
- Working as part of a team
- Counseling
- Promoting
- Coaching
- Reading
- Assembling
- Engineering
- Agriculture/forestry
- Finance
- Fundraising
- Translating
- Investigating
- Motivating
- Designing
- Performing
- Owning a store
- Politics
- Selling

The following exercise will help you further define your own areas of interests.

School Activities or Subjects You Liked Best:

_____

_____

_____

Extracurricular Activities or Events You Liked Best:

_____

_____

Work Experience or Tasks You Liked Best:

_____

_____

Community Projects or Events You Liked Best:

_____

_____

Recreational Activities You Liked Best:

_____

_____

Add any other areas that are important for you.

List the top four or five interests that you find yourself most frequently involved in:

1. _____

2. _____

3. _____

4. _____

5. _____

One theory that helps structure the career planning process is that of Dr. John Holland, who identified six categories or job families that are used to describe jobs. Holland assumed that workers could be loosely classified in these six groups, which describe personality types of workers. You can get a picture of where you fit into this structure from looking at the following clusters.

Realistic

- You enjoy physical, concrete structure work.
- You enjoy working with your hands.
- You have mechanical skills.
- You enjoy seeing the end product of your labors.

Investigative

- You enjoy solving problems and puzzles.
- You are a curious, analytic, and orderly thinker.
- You like using research skills.

Artistic

- You are an imaginative, expressive, and non-structured "ideas" person.
- You enjoy "right brain" activities, such as acting, writing, painting, and designing.

Social

- Educating and helping others is important to you.
- You enjoy working in settings like schools, social agencies, hospitals, religious organizations, or community services.
- You like to work with people to help and inform them.

Enterprising

- You are a friendly, sociable leader.
- You enjoy risk taking to gain recognition or power.
- You are comfortable in business, courtrooms, or political environments.
- You like to interact with others for your own gain.

Conventional

- You enjoy concrete tasks that are orderly, specific, and systematic.
- You are comfortable in financial environments and business settings.

No job or career can ever satisfy *all* of your interests. But you *can* strive to find areas that will take advantage of some of your strongest vocational interests. Of course, other interests can always be satisfied through volunteer work, hobbies, or recreational activities, which will serve to round out your life.

Check the areas that may be a vocational interest for you on the Holland List. To research the fields you've checked, begin with *The Occupational Outlook Handbook* in your college library or Career Center.

Realistic—includes skilled trades, technical, and some service occupations.

- Animal Service
- Athletics and Sports
- Protective Service
- Mechanical
- Manual and Skilled Trades
- Electronics
- Carpentry
- Nature/Outdoors Work

Investigative—includes scientific and some technical operations.

- Mathematics
- Biology
- Science Research
- Chemistry
- Medical Science
- Anthropology
- Geology

Artistic—includes artistic, media, music, and literary occupations.

- Stage Director
- Creative Artist
- Actor
- Writer
- Interior Designer
- Performer/Entertainer

Social—includes educational and social welfare occupations.

- Religious Activities
- Medical Service

- Community Service
- Education
- Counseling
- Case Worker
- Psychologist
- Speech Therapist

Enterprising—includes managerial, sales, and marketing occupations.

- Management/Supervision
- Law and Politics
- Producer
- Public Speaker
- Buyer
- Sales
- Business Executive
- Promoter

Conventional—includes office and clerical occupations.

- Office Worker
- Accounting
- Administrator
- Financial Analyst
- Banking
- Tax Expert
- Cost Estimator
- Food Service

Rank your three highest categories:

_____ Realistic

_____ Investigative

_____ Artistic

_____ Social

_____ Enterprising

_____ Conventional

1. I resemble the _____ type the most.

2. I resemble the _____ type next.

3. I resemble the _____ type next.

It's helpful to think about jobs as *environments* some of which are more hospitable and welcoming to some types of people than to others. Generally, people who find jobs and career paths that most closely match their type are expected to have the most job satisfaction.

You will need to research career possibilities that may be a good match for you. For each job title you are considering, think about the following questions.

- Do you have the necessary skills and abilities to do the job?

- If you do not, can you get the necessary knowledge and learn the skills?

- Can you afford the education and/or training you may need?

- Are you familiar with the lifestyle this occupation offers? Are you comfortable with it?

- Can you comfortably envision yourself in this career or industry?

Self-Assessment Summary

Increasing your own self-awareness is a critical first step in making your career choices. The self-assessment process is a never-ending one. As you grow and develop, so will your interests and abilities. From time to time you will need to reevaluate the items that are of true value and importance to you, so that you always have a clear picture of yourself as a worker. That way you will be able to do the best job of directing and managing your career.

As you grow and develop new interests, you will also want to develop new skills to help you get into new areas. Career plans can and *should* be reassessed at any point.

Fill in what you think makes the most sense for you *now*.

I would like my work life to reflect these values:

1. _____
2. _____
3. _____
4. _____
5. _____

My major work-related skills are:

1. _____
2. _____
3. _____
4. _____
5. _____

My principle interests are:

1. _____
2. _____
3. _____
4. _____
5. _____

I plan to research these career areas:

_____

_____

_____

The fields I am most seriously considering are:

_____

_____

My preference is _____, because _____

_____

_____

_____

In order to enter that field, I will need to:

1. _____
2. _____
3. _____

Dates I anticipate completing these goals:

1. _____
2. _____
3. _____

16

Career Exploration

The first step in exploring the wide range of career opportunities open to you is **research**. Learn to use the varied references available in your school or local library, such as *The Dictionary of Occupational Titles*, *The Occupational Outlook Handbook* (published by the U.S. Department of Labor), and the many books and pamphlets on careers ranging from architecture to zoology. Trade and professional associations are also excellent resources, as each industry tries to encourage young men and women to consider joining their ranks.

Collecting additional information from direct resources might include:

- Informational interviewing
- Talking with an instructor in the field
- Talking with people employed in the industry to get a picture of hiring needs
- Considering internships, cooperative educational opportunities, and part-time and summer jobs to get first-hand information

Many college placement offices now offer computerized career exploration services. DISCOVER is the computerized career guidance system for self-exploration of your interests, skills, abilities, and values. It also provides for an exploration of occupations.

The DISCOVER system can also be used to search for transfer institutions that may offer your field of occupational interest.

Career services professionals can also arrange for panels of industry experts, Career Fairs, and Career Days. Meet with your counselor to discuss what you'd like to learn more about. Allow department chairpersons and faculty to help arrange meetings and workshops with their own industry contacts.

A Wealth of Occupational Information at Your Fingertips!

There are many, many resources available for career exploration. Spend enough time in the library reviewing the available information on jobs, career paths, and industries.

To survey the field

American Almanac of Jobs and Salaries

Occupational Outlook Handbook

U.S. Industrial Outlook

Dictionary of Occupational Titles

State and country

County Directory of Business

Local Chamber of Commerce Directory

MacRae's State Industrial Directory

Statewide Job Opportunities

Large firms

Standard & Poor's Register of Corporations

Dun & Bradstreet's Million Dollar Directory

Moody's Industrial Manual

Value Line Investment Survey

College Placement Council Placement Annual

International

The Complete Guide to International Jobs

The Almanac of International Jobs and Careers

How to Get a Job in Europe

Directory of Overseas Summer Jobs

European Markets

International Careers

Periodicals

The Chronicle of Higher Education

Business Week

Forbes

Fortune Magazine

National Business Employment Weekly

Federal government

Federal Career Opportunities

U.S. Government Manual

How to Get A Federal Job

Specialty publications

Directory of Directories

Association Directories

Business Pages of the telephone book

Peterson's Guides

Directory of Executive Recruiters

Wonderful guides are also available that offer advice on getting jobs in major cities, such as New York, Chicago, Fort Worth/ Dallas, Miami, San Francisco, Washington, D.C., and Los Angeles.

VGM Careers Encyclopedia describes almost 200 careers, including specialized fields within occupations. And every two years the U.S. Department of Labor publishes a new edition of the *Occupational Outlook Handbook* (OOH). It describes the most popular occupations in the country, from A to Z. You will be able to research the nature of the work you are investigating, as well as the training and education requirements, salary and working conditions, the employment outlook, and even sources to refer to for additional information about the field. It's an informative and important career resource. Keep in mind that listed salary ranges are a national average and may not be precise for your specific locale.

17

Networking

Networking accounts for as much as 75 percent of job placements...but *what is it*? **Networking** simply means **using one's resources**—the people you know—to help you open the doors that will lead to a job. And it's the key to a successful job search. Networking is part of gathering information and job leads. It's a resource or a contact, a person with whom you develop a mutually beneficial relationship. Networking usually involves exchanging information and details with someone in an industry you are interested in. And it is considered very acceptable to turn to others for help. *They* probably did when they were establishing their own careers. Networking is one of the most powerful job-search tools, and you should learn to be comfortable with it. You can use it to:

- Exchange information, ideas, and contacts
- Give and get advice and support
- Increase your confidence
- Locate internships and job leads
- Develop mentors
- Form both professional and personal long-term relationships

Most people are delighted to be helpful—particularly young professionals on their way up the career ladder who are often flattered to be asked for their advice and counsel. If people are unavailable or uninterested, they will let you know. So: Put your feelings of timidity about asking for assistance aside. Talking with a seasoned professional may feel intimidating to you, particularly if you feel you have little to return or share in the way of industry advice. Therefore, start your networking with peers. Chances are, you'll feel more confident when you *do* encounter those with more experience and time in the industry. Friends from college, colleagues on past jobs, family members, and others can be part of your initial network. Use them for ideas, for encouragement, and for support.

The more you practice networking, the more easily you will do it. Soon you'll begin to see the results. You need to keep the networking process alive throughout your career. Contacts will give you information that may lead to interviews. Interviews can lead to jobs—and jobs develop careers!

How to Get Started

Before beginning to network, identify your goals for your job search. You must know:

- The kind of work you want to do
- The industries you prefer to work in

Your career counselor may be able to help you target people in the field that you want to enter. Alumni are generally eager to become active in working with undergraduates in this way. Entry-level workers often get started on career paths with the help of people already in the industry. People who are already successful in their field are important contacts for you. They probably enjoy what they do and are often pleased to share their information and leads with others who are just starting out. You should aim to be in touch with people who have made things happen in your field of interest.

Other possible contacts include:

- Relatives
- Friends
- Neighbors

- Teachers
- Classmates
- Sorority and fraternity contacts
- Colleagues from work or internship situations

You can raise your own visibility with prospective employers and other key industry representatives by attending Career Fairs at your college. This is always an important networking opportunity. Make sure you check with your placement department to get dates and places of all such events on campus.

Always keep a supply of résumés as well as neatly printed **business cards** with you. This will speed along the networking process as you will always be prepared to exchange cards or give your résumé to those you meet in business settings. You could even include a business card in any correspondence you send, so the receiver will add it to her or his professional files.

Consider joining clubs and organizations relating to your major or your areas of career interest. Attend meetings and get involved in regional or national conferences. You'll be able to hear and meet notable industry speakers at many of these events. Major employers and their recruiters attend these conferences to scout for strong, entry-level candidates. Keep in mind as well that any part-time job, co-op assignment, or internship experience is an excellent opportunity to meet people in industry and have them view you as a prospective new hire.

Keep your networking skills alive and you'll always have the ability to identify new career opportunities and interesting career contacts, even when you are employed. Relying on people as a career resource is not only very *acceptable*...it's very *smart*.

The Networking Process

Once you identify people to contact, you must develop and fine tune how you present yourself to them. Practice how you would introduce yourself when mingling with other professionals and workers at business meetings, trade shows, and conferences. You can actually start by writing a brief script for yourself. It might sound like this: "Hello. I'm Roslyn Dolber. I've just graduated from _____ College with a degree in Advertising Design. I'm in the midst of a job search for an entry-level position in the graphics field. I'd love to start working for a magazine or newspaper doing paste-ups and layouts."

Try to be as specific as you can, so the listener is immediately clear about your interests and the direction of your job search. Keep reviewing and revising your introduction as your job objectives and career goals become more focused.

When networking, you'll need to discuss your interest in entering the particular field and your background and qualifications. Your emphasis should be on getting specific job market information from each contact. A contact can provide job leads or give you access to others in the field who may provide you with tips, strategies, and job referrals. Build up your contacts to gradually increase the circle of people who can be helpful—either with specific job leads or referrals to other prospective employers. *All* the information you receive is valuable. Be gracious in thanking your contacts for their time and their information. This is *definitely* the right time for thank-you notes. Down the road, once you are established in the labor market, don't forget that you'll be called upon to do the same for the next group of beginners in your field. And remember: Maintain a positive attitude but be *reasonable* in your networking. Don't ask for too much at one time from any one resource.

When you develop your networking plan, you are simply identifying areas that you need to research and determining who you will use to help you get that information. Set up an easy-to-follow plan. It could look like this:

Networking plan

Job/career you want details about _____

Industries you want details about _____

Identify who you think could be helpful:

Employers in the field _____

_____

_____

Contacts _____

_____

Referral sources _____

_____

Professional organizations _____

_____

Conferences, trade or industrial shows, business meetings to attend to begin networking _____

_____

Action plan for the week of _____

- Make _____ phone contacts
- Schedule _____ appointments/meetings
- Attend _____ industry events
- Send _____ letters to potential contacts
- Meet _____ new people who are in the field

The more people you contact, the greater your chances are for a successful job search. Your networking contacts can serve as your publicity team!

Summary: Essentials of Networking

- Networking is a mutual give-and-take of information—advice, leads, and support.
- As a beginner, you'll need to get more information and support than you'll be able to give.
- Contact as many people who you feel can be helpful or who can direct you to others who can be helpful.
- Keep notes and follow up with each lead that you get.
- Always thank people each time they assist you.
- Develop your own lists of friends, alumni, professional groups, professors, career counselors, and others who can serve as future resources.

- Be patient. The results of your efforts may not come immediately. The payoff may be weeks or even *months* away.

- Share information generously. People will be quick to decide that you are only a "taker" if you are unwilling to return information, leads, or resources whenever you can. Networking is a two-way process. Helping others is a critical part of building a networking relationship.

18

Informational Interviews

Informational interviews are designed for one reason only: *to gather information*. An informational interview is a chance to collect information about a job, career, or an industry that interests you. It is *not* a request for a job. The information you acquire will also prepare you to be a well-informed candidate.

In an informational interview, *you* decide which kind of firm and what level of employee you'd like to talk with. Informational interviews are an important means of **networking** and an excellent way to develop a list of contacts for the future. And, of course, you also gain current details about a particular field of work. Treat these interviews with care. The person you talk to may well turn out to be an important source of valuable information and other contacts.

Getting Started

Target people in a company or industry that you would like to enter and arrange for an informational interview. Phone the person who you feel may be a resource for you and explain that you are researching the industry, a particular job, or even that firm. Ask if they are available to meet with you. Be prepared to be flexible and adjust your calendar to meet at their convenience. Busy people may even suggest a telephone interview if they cannot set other time aside. You should not reject such an offer.

Remember, this is *not* a job interview! It's your chance to speak with someone who is employed in the field of your choice who can give you details about the nature of the work, the educational requirements, and the opportunities for growth in the industry. Be ready to ask for information relating to trends in the field, attitudes, new technologies and developments, and so on. Try to get the names of other people you could contact. Ask the people you meet with how they got started, what their daily routine is, what they like and dislike about their assignment, and their thoughts on the industry. Ask if their duties have changed, how, what their responsibilities are, what skills are needed to succeed at their level, and what the best educational program might be for someone who is eager to enter the field. You might even ask if the economy has affected business, and their thoughts on any current trends.

Discuss current career opportunities in the field, as well as typical entry-level positions and career paths. Try to get advice on how to become a part of the industry.

In an informational interview, you can:

- Gather information about career paths, job titles, and the work environment
- Talk about current issues, trends, or developments in the industry
- Develop a list of others in the field with whom you might arrange informational interviews
- Learn about educational requirements, training, and industry expectations

At the end of your meeting, don't forget to ask if there are others in the field that you might contact to continue your research. "Could you suggest one or two other people who might also be willing to meet with me?" is a fine way to get a response. Do make it clear that you are *not* asking for a referral to a job, but for further information. Always bear in mind that the purpose of this type of meeting is for you to get valuable information and **feedback**.

Because you will be dealing with busy professionals, keep your meetings brief. Suggest early morning breakfast meetings or end-of-the-day appointments, so you don't interfere with your contact's hectic work schedule.

The following questions will help you begin gathering information:

- Could you please describe your major job responsibilities?
- What is the career path for someone in your position?
- What education or experience would best prepare me to enter this field?
- How did you get started in this industry?
- How did you prepare for it?
- Can you describe what a typical day is like?
- Can you tell me about the potential for growth and advancement on the job?
- What are the future trends in this industry?
- What skills should I be developing now?
- How is your firm structured? To whom do you report? Do you supervise others? Will you have supervisory responsibilities in the future?
- If you were hiring someone for your own job, what qualities would you seek?
- What do you enjoy about your occupation?
- What are the working conditions like on your job?
- What are the starting salaries for entry-level workers?
- What other career paths are closely related to yours?

Always send a thank-you note after an informational interview. Send a follow-up note after you have spoken with their suggested contacts. Not only is this a polite gesture, but it reinforces your professionalism. A thank-you note is a good way to be remembered. A brief, but sincere, statement describing how you benefited from the meeting will serve you well.

You may even want to keep a diary or journal to jot down brief notes after each interview. Include all the new information you gained and the names of new contacts. This will keep you organized and come in handy when you send out your letters of thanks.

Sample Letter Requesting an Informational Interview

November 2, 1995
Ms. Elise Bennett
Executive Vice President
Amazing Company
1234 Harbor Lane
West Palm Beach, FL 34567

Dear Ms. Bennett,

I am writing at the suggestion of our mutual contact (or friend, acquaintance, etc.) Ms. Amy Chin, who has known me for the past several summers (or any other information that will establish that contact's connection to the reader). She has recommended you as a source of information relative to my career goals.

I would welcome the chance to meet with you to explore the current marketplace and how I might best use my skills and abilities in entering the publishing field. I appreciate any time you may have available in your busy schedule. I will call your office next week to set up a brief meeting at your convenience. I look forward to talking with you.*

Sincerely,

Sign your name
Type your name
Address
City, state and zip code

* If you enclose your résumé, add this sentence: I am enclosing my résumé for your reference.

Sample Thank-You Note

November 23, 1995

Dear Ms. Bennett,
    Thank you for the information and advice you offered when we met yesterday. It was most generous of you to take time from your busy work schedule to share your thinking and to provide me with additional contacts within the publishing field.
    I will be following up on the leads you suggested, and I will be pleased to keep you informed of my progress. (Make specific reference to something that was discussed or recommended during the meeting to personalize your note and remind her of the visit).
    Again, many thanks for encouraging my career goals. Our meeting was valuable and I appreciate your support.
Sincerely,

Sign your name
Type your name

Summary: Learning from Your Contacts

Informational interviews will provide you with a basic knowledge and understanding of the work world and the industry or career that interests you. Use the time you spend in informational interviewing to learn:

- Nature of the work
- Necessary education or training
- Working conditions
- Salary ranges
- Location of employment—local, national, or international
- Travel or relocation involved
- Advantages and disadvantages of the profession
- Related occupations
- General ideas about the future of the field

19

Cover Letters and Résumés

When recruiters or interviewers are faced with a stack of cover letters and résumés, they scan each piece of paper to weed out those candidates that seem unlikely. They look for applicants who build a strong case for themselves. *You will need to look good on paper!*

The information that you convey to the reader of *your* cover letter and résumé should certainly make it clear that you have the **skills** and **background** to do the job. But the information should also suggest a great **interest** in the job and the organization, that you are an enthusiastic and willing worker! These written materials must give the reader a sense that you know what you want—what job, towards what career goal, and in what industry. Make it to the point. Omit descriptive clutter and detailed descriptions. Focus on your strengths and accomplishments and show just how well qualified you are!

Your cover letter should tell the reader

- Why you are writing
- What specific job interests you
- What your qualifications are
- How you will follow up with the reader

Your résumé should tell the reader

- Who you are
- What job you are seeking
- What you have done
- What you can do
- What you know

And it should also

- Serve to get you an interview
- Introduce your education and skills
- Be a reminder of you after the interview is over

> Outstanding cover letters and résumés will get your reader's attention!

The Cover Letter

A cover letter must *always* accompany your résumé, whether it is mailed or faxed. It serves to introduce you to the reader, who is usually an interviewer or a recruiter. It explains why your résumé has been sent. Your cover letter should convince the reader to review your résumé and consider *you* for a job interview.

If you can find out who is responsible for hiring at a particular firm, check for the correct title and spelling of that person's name and address the cover letter to him or her. If you are not able to get this information, address your cover letter to the Director of Human Resources at the company.

Your cover letter should not exceed three to four paragraphs and should never be longer than one typewritten page. Aim to keep the letter simple. Avoid repeating the information that is given in your résumé. The person reading your cover letter should be able to quickly learn of your interest in applying for a specific position. Hopefully, your cover letter will persuade him or her to read your attached résumé for more details about you.

Personalize the cover letter so that each one you write is specifically geared to the firm you are approaching. Make it clear in your cover letter what you can offer the company and what interests you about the job. Be sure that spelling and punctuation are correct. Neatly type your letter on white paper, and don't forget to sign your name just above the line where it is typed!

Never use photocopied letters. Each one you send must be an original. Your cover letter should be personal and should encourage a prospective employer to want to learn more about your background and your future goals. A thoughtful and clearly written cover letter will introduce you and your résumé to the reader.

Review the following samples of typical cover letters. Note that the reason it's being sent is clearly stated in the first paragraph. This is the place to identify the position you're applying for and mention how you learned about it. A brief statement describing your background and why you feel you qualify for the job comes next. Close on a positive note, expressing your interest in arranging for an interview. You can do all this in just a few paragraphs. You need to spend as much time and effort in composing a standout cover letter as you do creating a résumé. It's the first impression that you convey to potential employers, interviewers, and recruiters, and you want it to be a great one!

A clear and effective cover letter saves the reader the time of searching through each résumé. Sent along with your résumé, it reinforces how well you match the job requirements.

Cover Letter How-to

The parts of a cover letter are simple. In addition to your own address, telephone, and fax number —if you have one—you need the date, and the name and address of the person and the organization you are applying to. Remember: All your cover letter needs is *three* paragraphs.

> your current address
> city, state, zip code
> telephone and/or fax number
>
> date
>
> interviewer's name
> title
> company

street address
city, state, zip code

Dear Ms. or Mr. (include interviewer's name),

First paragraph

- Explain why you are writing.
- Tell what you want.
- Tell how you heard of the job opening.

Second paragraph

- Highlight one or two key qualifications that are in your résumé that will be of interest to the reader.
- Select your strongest points that are relevant to the firm or the job.
- Explain why you are interested in the position, the firm, or the industry.
- If you have related training or experience, briefly state it.

Third paragraph

- Indicate that your résumé is attached or enclosed.
- Request an interview. State when you will call to arrange it, rather than ending on a vague, open-ended note.

Yours truly,
sign your name
type your name

Cover Letter "Do's"

Follow these simple guidelines when you compose your cover letter.

- Write an original cover letter for every firm you mail or fax your résumé to.
- Date it.

- Include your address, telephone, and fax number in the heading.
- The correct place for your name is at the end. Sign your name just above your typewritten name.
- Use good-quality white or off-white paper, and matching business-size envelopes.
- Address your letter to a specific person.
- Make sure the title and spelling of the name are correct.
- Follow the instructions on the job lead or the classified ad.
- Whenever possible, research the company before you compose the cover letter to familiarize yourself with the firm's services, products, policies, and so on.
- Limit it to three or four paragraphs, which should fill only one typewritten page.
- Always close with a polite request for a specific interview.
- Check for neat layout and overall appearance.
- Proofread for grammatical, spelling, and typing errors.
- Remember that your cover letter is viewed as a sample of your writing skill.
- Have another person proofread it after you do.
- Keep copies of everything you send.
- Follow up at the time you have stated you will do so.

Cover Letter "Don'ts"

- Don't tell *everything* in the letter. Be concise. Your résumé should convey what the reader needs to know and what you want to save for the interview.
- Don't include your photograph. You'll be interviewed based on your qualifications, not your appearance.
- Don't use "Dear Sir," "Dear Madame," or "To Whom It May Concern." The *only* exception is when you respond to a classified ad that might only list a box number. In that case, use "Dear Employer."

- Don't include your name in the heading of the letter. And *don't* use nicknames. You can always let the interviewer know what you prefer to be called when you meet.

- Don't be whimsical or cute. Attempt to be straightforward and businesslike. Be professional in your writing as well as in your behavior.

- Don't forget to follow up. Mark your calendar and be *sure* you make the next contact when you indicated that you would.

Sample Cover Letter

32 West Walk
Dunewood, New York 11734
(516) 555-0000

May 1, 1996

Mr. Alan Ira
Personnel Director
Alan's Menswear
25 Main Street
Fair Harbor, New York 11706

Dear Mr. Ira,

I am most interested in applying for the position of store manager that you listed in the campus Employment Office at Long Island University.

My part-time and summer sales experience in the retail field, plus my coursework as a Fashion Merchandising major, have given me an excellent background for the opening. I have read about your firm's highly regarded training program and I am eager to learn more about it.

I look forward to a career in retail management upon my graduation. My résumé is enclosed for your review.

I will call your office next week to set up an appointment for an interview at your convenience.

Yours truly,

Sign your name
Type your mane

Sample Cover Letter

1939 Gull Walk
Atlantic City, N.J. 08879
(201) 556-3980

May 1, 1996

Sonya Ruiz
Ruiz Productions
47 West 37 Street
New York, N.Y. 10016

Dear Ms. Ruiz,

Dr. Peter Miller, my Advertising Design professor at the State University of New York, recommended that I contact you regarding the job opening for a junior designer.

My enclosed résumé details the related coursework I have taken during the past four years in college, including my internship at The Masters Agency, where I worked closely with the senior Art Director. My portfolio includes many samples of my paste-up, layout, and design projects, one of which placed second in the Statewide Design Competition.

I am familiar with the creative work your production company is known for and I would be delighted to meet with you. I will call your office the week of May 17th, to arrange for a convenient interview time.

Yours truly,

Sign your name
Type your name

The Résumé

A résumé is your ticket to a job interview! It's your marketing tool. It's your advertisement for yourself. It's your way of selling yourself to prospective employers to get an interview.

A *great* résumé is one that gives a brief—but effective—summary of your qualifications. It should reflect your experiences, education, accomplishments, skills, and interests. And it must serve to *attract* and *impress* a prospective employer. Its purpose is to create an invitation for a job interview. It can't *guarantee* you a job, but it can open the door for you, allowing you to meet with a recruiter, an interviewer, or an employer. It is an important screening tool widely used by industry. You'll want to make yours the best possible representation of yourself.

Getting Started

To begin, you need to think about your background and your past experiences. What skills and qualifications can you offer an employer? This is the point the time you've spent in your own self-assessment pays off well. Don't forget to work with your college's Career Counseling department if you need assistance with the assessment or the résumé writing process.

You will need to select a format for your résumé. Choose either **chronological** or **functional**, depending upon which will be the most effective for you. Stay with whatever format style you choose throughout the entire résumé. You do not need to design a new résumé for each job you apply for. One all-purpose model usually works very well for beginners. But you'll want to select the résumé style that is best suited to your experiences.

Chronological résumé

- A popular choice for beginning workers
- Easy to read
- Clearly details your school and work history
- Dates are listed to give employers a quick picture of your background

Functional résumé

- Highlights your skills, rather than school or work history
- Dates are not emphasized, so readers work a bit harder to put your background together
- Often suited for people with strong skills that might not be highlighted in a chronological format

Combination résumé

- Uses features of both the functional and chronological résumé styles
- Skills are described, but jobs and school experience are also detailed

Begin by drawing up a rough draft, using the categories that will be described. Include everything that you think may be relevant. Then continue to work on additional drafts to edit out unnecessary information. Refine and polish it to a one-page personal advertisement for yourself that highlights your best attributes and experiences. Use **action words** that are powerful, such as *organized*, *designed*, *implemented*, *led*, and *achieved*. Review the sample résumés in this chapter to get an idea of what an acceptable beginner's résumé might look like.

Spend as much time as you can designing your résumé. It must reflect *you*. When you have a final draft that you feel comfortable with, ask a career counselor, faculty member, or advisor to review it with you.

Next, type up your résumé and have it duplicated. Aim for a neat and professional look, rather than breaking the bank on the most expensive paper available or the priciest printing job. Pay attention to the layout and how it looks on the printed page. Keep in mind that if you end up faxing your résumé, no one will be able to tell that you have spent a fortune on quality paper.

How to Build a Great Résumé

The résumés of many recent college graduates and entry-level workers tend to look very similar. Your job should be to make yours stand out by tailoring it to the job you are seeking. There is no one format that appeals to every recruiter, so choose the form that most appeals to you. Remember, the chronological résumé lists your background in sequential order, outlining the most recent events first and working backwards. It's most commonly used by recent college graduates, who tend to have limited work experience, because it can easily emphasize responsibilities, skills, accomplishments, and academic honors. It's also easy to prepare.

If you're lucky enough to have had past work experience and strong areas of expertise, you may want to consider a functional style résumé. This focuses on your skills and summarizes your work history. It can also help you downplay a poor school record or gaps in your employment.

Write the first draft of your résumé yourself. You may not be able to do the final, polished edition, but as you organize your thoughts and put your school, work, and volunteer history down in writing, you are preparing information that you will need and use at every interview that you have.

Your college Career Center may offer a résumé writing workshop or a résumé critique service. You can always resort to a professional résumé service, but these are often very expensive and you may end up with a document that doesn't read or sound like you. Attempt to do as much work as you can on your own résumé. A well-thought-out and effective résumé will be your reward!

Putting It All Together

Right from the beginning, when you sit down to write a draft, pay attention to using plenty of **action words**. Action words will make your résumé come alive—and make *you* look good!

Emphasize your **accomplishments**. This is *not* the time to be modest. Without bragging or exaggerating, state your accomplishments and your achievements.

Be **specific**. It's more impressive to state "increased sales over 35 percent" rather than simply stating "good selling skills."

Avoid **negatives**. If you think that it's important for a prospective employer to know something that may reflect in a negative way on you, omit it from your résumé and raise that issue during the interview. At that time you will be able to discuss it privately, and in the manner that you choose. Don't forget that many people may see your résumé once you mail or fax it out. It is *not* a confidential document.

Be aware of the **layout**. Make your résumé easy to read. Use bullets (•), BOLD TYPE, or *italics* to help break up the copy. Short crisp statements are easier to read than lengthy ones. You do not need to write in complete sentences. It's fine to eliminate the word "I," as the reader will assume you are referring to yourself.

Make sure you are generous with **margins**. Leave lots of space on the page—it's easier on the eyes and it will look good. Interviewers and recruiters who have to sort through dozens of résumés each day will gravitate towards those that look neat, professional, and easy-to-read.

Proofread, proofread, proofread. Errors are simply *not* acceptable. Don't mark yourself as a sloppy worker. You ruin your chances of being called in for an interview. It's wise to have another person proof your final version so that errors you didn't see will be caught by another pair of eyes.

Keep it **businesslike**. You don't have to spend a fortune on top-quality paper, but go for the best that your budget allows. White or off-white paper is universally acceptable. Hold off on pastel shades or bold colors. You are *not* making a fashion statement. And make sure every copy of your résumé is of letter quality. This is no time to skimp on duplicating processes. You can easily have your résumé prepared on a word processor with a laser printer. That is very acceptable and even allows you to revise and update your résumé as needed.

Summary: Designing Your Résumé

- Prepare your own résumé drafts.

- Use short statements and phrases rather than full sentences.

- Begin statements with action verbs and avoid the pronoun "I."

- Expect to write several drafts until you arrive at a final version.

- If you include a **career objective**, keep it specific and focused.

- An oversimplified goal, such as "any entry job," is not acceptable.

- Be concise. Keep the résumé to one page.

- Make it easy-to-read, with lots of wide margins and space on the page.

- Select your résumé format and be consistent.

- Highlight accomplishments and achievements.

- Make the most of volunteer work or participation in student government or other student activities on campus, especially if you have little or no past work experience.

- Use columns, capital letters, underlining, or bullets to emphasize items.

- Avoid negative statements.

- Be honest and accurate about everything that you include.

- Proofread it more than once, and then have someone else proof it to catch errors you missed.

Avoid These Common Résumé Mistakes

- Don't type the word RÉSUMÉ at the top of the page.

- Don't abbreviate. Spell out "Bachelor of Arts degree," rather than using "BA degree."

- Don't use nicknames. Save that for the college scene.

- Don't exaggerate or overstate your qualifications.

- Don't make handwritten corrections.

- Don't put a date on the résumé.

- Don't include your photograph.

- Don't indicate personal data, such as race, religion, or political affiliation.

- Don't include your salary expectations or your salary on past jobs.

- Don't describe the reasons you've left jobs or changed schools. You can always discuss these items at the interview.

The Parts of a Résumé

Heading

Include your full name, complete address with zip code, telephone number, and fax number, if applicable.

Job objective

Identify the job you are targeting. Compose a clearly stated one- or two-liner, such as:

- Position as a marketing assistant in the fashion field
- Entry job as an editorial assistant in book publishing
- Receptionist in a medical office
- Physical therapist for a community health agency
- Entry-level worker in the hotel/hospitality industry

Try to have your job objective answer these questions:

- What do you want to do?
- Where do you want to do it?
- At what level of job responsibility?

If you don't want to limit yourself to one type of position, you do not need to include a job objective on your résumé.

Education

For beginning workers, this section usually preceeds Work History. It you have an unusual work history, simply put the education category after it. Summarize your school background and indicate your highest degree, major, program of study, and the name of the college. List dates. If your G.P.A. is 3.0 or better, include it along with any academic honors or scholarships. There is no need to make mention of high- school graduation dates or honors.

Extracurricular activities

List your participation in student leadership organizations, student government, clubs, honor societies, athletic teams, and any other groups.

Employment

List the dates, the name of the firm, and the position you held. Use short statements to summarize your duties and any special projects or assignments you completed. Indicate any contributions you made to the department or the unit. Include part-time, summer, and internship jobs, and any volunteer work.

Optional information

Use your judgment to decide if you need to "flesh out" the page by including any additional information. If your page is filled with solid data, there is no need to pad it.

Course highlights

Include several lines or two columns itemizing specialized or particularly relevant courses you have taken, especially if you have limited work experience.

Affiliations

Note your membership or participation in any professional organization. If you've held leadership or administrative positions, be sure to include that information.

Interests/hobbies

Use this section as an opportunity to show the reader how well-rounded you are, if space permits. Anything relating to your career objective is a plus!

Skills

You can list your skills after detailing your work experience. Don't make subjective statements. Instead, focus on factual statements of real abilities and talent, such as "computer literate," "fluent in French and Hebrew," "pilot's license," and so on.

References

You do *not* need to include the line "References will be furnished upon request." It is assumed that all reference requests will *indeed* be furnished by you. Never list the names and telephone numbers of references on your résumé. This is to be supplied to an interviewer on a separate sheet of paper once you have the permission of those people you'd like to include.

Action Verbs for a Powerful Résumé

These words attract the attention of the reader, and give an active sense of your skills and abilities.

accomplished	evaluated	planned
achieved	expanded	prepared
advised	expedited	presented
analyzed	exceeded	processed
appraised	facilitated	produced
approved	formulated	programmed
arranged	founded	provided
assisted	gathered	published
chaired	generated	reduced
checked	handled	reinforced
collected	improved	reorganized
compiled	implemented	repaired
completed	increased	researched
computed	initiated	resolved
conducted	instructed	revamped
constructed	interpreted	reviewed
consulted	interviewed	revised
coordinated	introduced	rewrote
copied	invented	sold
counseled	launched	set up
created	led	streamlined
delegated	maintained	served as
demonstrated	managed	supervised
developed	monitored	supported
directed	motivated	surveyed
distributed	negotiated	taught
edited	operated	trained
eliminated	organized	updated
equipped	participated	upgraded
established	performed	utilized
estimated	persuaded	

Rating Your Résumé

Once you have written your final résumé draft, rate it against the items listed here. Are there areas that need strengthening? You should rewrite your résumé until you are satisfied that you are presenting the *best* picture of yourself, your experiences, and your accomplishments.

Final draft checklist

Overall Appearance and Layout

_____ Does it look professional?

_____ Is it neatly typed with good margins?

_____ Do key points you want to highlight stand out?

Length

_____ Is the information condensed effectively?

Relevance

_____ Have you edited out all unrelated items?

Writing Style

_____ Is it easy to get a picture of your strengths and qualifications?

Action Orientation

_____ Have you started phrases with action verbs as often as possible?

Specificity

_____ Have you avoided general statements and focused on specific accomplishments and experiences?

Completeness

_____ Is all vital information listed?

_____ Have you included all relevant details?

Sample of a Chronological Résumé

Philip Zucker
2898 Jackson Street
San Francisco, California 94121
(415) 416-5555 telephone
(415) 416-3333 fax

OBJECTIVE
Entry-level showroom sales position for a menswear apparel manufacturer.

EDUCATION
The Fashion Institution of Technology, San Francisco, CA
Associate in Applied Science degree, June 1996
Fashion Merchandising major

Related coursework:
* Introduction to Fashion   * Advertising Promotion
* Computer Usage I & II   * Fashion Merchandising
* Product Development   * Consumer Motivation
* International Markets   * Fashion Publicity

HONORS AND AWARDS
Dean's List, Spring 1996
Macy's Scholarship, 1995 and 1996

WORK HISTORY
1995–present   J.C. Penney, San Francisco, CA
                        Sales Associate, part-time
                        • Assist customers in mens' apparel department
                        • Coordinate and accessorize purchases upon request
                        • Keep stock inventory and maintain floor displays
                        • Developed strong customer following and increased sales over 15 percent during 1995–1996 holiday season.

Summers 1994–1995   Duffy's Taverna, Palo Alto, CA
                        Waiter
                        • Served dinner clientele of up to 50 guests per night
                        • Frequently worked double shifts to assist in peak periods

SKILLS
Expert in WordPerfect 5.1 and IBM Retail Information Systems

Sample of a Chronological Résumé

Mark Bennett • 18 White Birch Lane • Moab, Utah 84747 • 801 123-5555

OBJECTIVE	Seeking entry management position utilizing organizational abilities, supervisory experience, and interpersonal skills.
EDUCATION	Loa State University, Loa, Utah Bachelor of Science degree, 1996 Business Management Major, Psychology Minor Related Courses: Advanced Managerial Theory Business Case Studies Statistics I & II Principles of Supervision Organizational Development
HONORS AND ACHIEVEMENTS	• All-State Debating Team Runner-Up, 1994 • Dean's List for two semesters • Financed 75 percent of all educational expenses with part-time and summer work in related positions.
EXPERIENCE Summers 1994– 1995	Assistant Manager—Forever Flowers • Supervised two employees • Responsible for ordering all supplies, in excess of $3,000 weekly • Handled new advertising promotion for summer and holiday season • Doubled membership in Flower of the Month Club
Part-time 1995–1996	Manager's Assistant—The Goldsmith • General assistant to store manager of high-volume fine jewelry retail store • Organized Christmas sales promotion, resulting in 15 percent increase in sales • Developed liaison with local colleges to promote sales of graduation rings on campus
ACTIVITIES	American Management Association, Student Chapter Sierra Club member Literacy Volunteers of America
INTERESTS	Hiking, Rock Climbing, Conversational Spanish

Sample of a Functional Résumé

GLORIA CHIN
1814 Deluth Parkway
Woodside, New York 11377
(718) 839-5555

EDUCATION	The Laboratory School, Burlington, Vermont Associate of Business degree, June 1996 Merchandising Major

* Dean's List, Spring 1996
* Treasurer of Merchandising Society, 1994–1995

Related Courses Included: Introduction to Business; Advertising & Promotion; Computers for Business; Public Relations for the Fashion Industry; Product Development.

EXPERIENCE & ACCOMPLISHMENTS

SALES. Developed loyal customer base in three menswear designer departments. Responsible for 15 percent increase in holiday sales. Earned "Employee of the Month" award, October 1996—first time ever for a part-time worker.

COMMUNICATIONS. Designed customer satisfaction survey. Tallied and coordinated 640 responses. Results incorporated into a new training procedure.

WORK HISTORY

The Gap, Burlington, Vermont
Part-time sales associate (1996–present)

Assist customers, help coordinate and accessorize purchases, responsible for all floor displays and stock. Handle cash register, help close out at end of shift. Responsible for all special orders.

HOBBIES & INTERESTS

Expert photographer with own printing and developing equipment. Fluent in French. Have traveled across U.S.A.

Summary: A Résumé That Will Work for You

- Do your own writing.
- Keep it brief and to the point. Don't exceed one page.
- Stress accomplishments and responsibilities.
- Use powerful action verbs.
- Give specific examples whenever possible.
- Use short, positive statements.
- Be honest. Don't exaggerate or embellish.
- Don't abbreviate.
- Don't include salary expectations, personal data, or a photograph.
- Be sure it looks great and is easy-to-read.

Remember to keep a log of all the people to whom you have sent your cover letter and résumé, so you can easily recognize their name and firm when you are contacted. It will also help remind you when you need to make follow-up calls or contacts.

20

Preparing for Your Job Search

Finding a job is **hard work**. Your first serious job search may be one of the most difficult assignments you have encountered. Unlike school, you'll have no faculty members monitoring your performance and letting you know how you're doing. Your success will largely depend on you alone. But once you have mastered some basic job hunting techniques, you'll have the thrill of getting your foot in the door of an industry of your choice—and earning your first paycheck. These are just some of the rewards for your efforts as you begin your climb up the career ladder.

Getting Ready

Regardless of when you leave school or at what point you begin to look for work, you will probably find stiff competition for entry-level jobs. Finding the job that will be a good fit for you is real work. Plan to seriously extend all of the energy and effort it requires. So be ready to:

- Spend each week actively involved in your job search
- Aim for at least one interview per day

- Set time aside for making phone calls, doing research, networking, writing notes, reviewing ads, and meeting with your career counselor or other professionals
- Let faculty members know that you are available
- Review each interview to practice stronger answers in the areas where you fell short
- Continue your networking activities throughout your job hunt
- Take advantage of every work-related opportunity, such as workshops, seminars, and career fairs
- Get together with other job seekers to share information and leads
- Keep in mind all of the fine skills you have and can offer an employer
- Develop a positive attitude
- Remain persistent and committed

Does this sound like you?

- Little or no interview research and practice?
- Overconfident about your abilities?
- Poor communication skills?
- Undecided or vague about career goals?
- Unrealistic expectations about your beginning position?
- Feeling your prospective boss owes you something so that you can move ahead quickly?

Before you can go forward with your job hunt, you must make an effort to correct those attitudes that will limit your potential success—and happiness. *Don't* become a part of the group of job applicants that employers complain about. These are people who:

- Have unrealistic work expectations and career aspirations
- Have weak interpersonal skills
- Have poor communication skills

- Have an arrogant attitude
- Overestimate their own abilities
- Lack motivation and commitment
- Submit poorly prepared cover letters and résumés
- Have not practiced their interviewing techniques

Maximize Your Opportunities

Make the most of your situation by strengthening those skills and attitudes that will help you succeed in your job search for a position in the field of your choice.

Communication skills

- Writing
- Public speaking
- Listening
- Reading

Interpersonal skills

- Leadership
- Managing or supervising
- Negotiating
- Teaching

Personal skills

- Self-management
- Time management
- Self-assessment of your own abilities

Informational skills

- Organizing
- Coordinating

- Researching
- Problem-solving
- Budget management

Computer Literacy

Computers are here to stay! Nearly every segment of the business world relies on computers, and will steadily continue to do so. If you still cannot handle basic PC functions, such as word processing, spreadsheets, and databases, your *immediate* plan should be to correct this. If you do not understand how computers function, you will have a difficult time in most industries. This weak spot may seriously affect your ability to move along in your chosen career path. *Remedy the situation now*!

It's your job to be computer literate.

Marketing yourself in a tough job market

Develop marketing skills to sell yourself to prospective employers. Then systematically attempt to work on your marketing plan. You might develop a weekly plan that looks something like this:

- Send résumé and cover letter to 50 firms listed in industry directory
- Respond to all classified ads for this week
- List with two new employment agencies
- Call my career counselor at college on Monday
- Follow up with calls back to at least two interviewers
- Try to generate four new interviews for this week
- Continue networking
- Attend Alumni Association Fundraiser on Wednesday

21

The Job Interview

The all-important job interview allows the employer to learn about you, but it is also the time for you to learn about the company and decide if you would want to work there. Skilled interviewers can learn a great deal about you from your résumé, your appearance, and the way in which you respond to questions. They can also read the subtle signals you communicate in the twenty or thirty minutes typically spent in an interview session.

Be prepared, however, to encounter interviewers who are not very experienced or comfortable with their hiring role. This is one of the many reasons why you need to be ready for interviews. Some will run smoothly, and some will feel awkward and slow moving. No matter how pleased you are with the outcome of an interview, chances are that each one will serve as a building block for you. If you take the time to thoughtfully reflect on the pros and cons of every contact with an interviewer, changing the areas where your performance was weak, you can truly improve your interviewing skills.

Everyone's first interview is a near disaster, but by the fifth, sixth, or tenth interview you will know what to expect and what questions need to have more focused or specific answers. You can pinpoint the areas in which you need to do more research. You can also learn what aspects of your body language needs more attention.

Advance Preparation Really Works!

Job applicants who are hired may not always be the most quali-fied candidates! But you can be sure that they are the most qual-ified at selling themselves. Use the time you have with each interviewer to convey the very best about yourself. It is your gold-en opportunity to convince the interviewer that you are the right person to fill that particular job opening. What you say, how you say it, the tone of your voice, the smile on your face, your pos-ture—they are all part of selling yourself during this anxious event.

To get a sense of how you come across to others, try to role play. This type of practice is important. It is used by large re-cruiting firms that deal with business executives, and it's prac-ticed in college campus Placement Centers. It will help you become more natural and relaxed in your responses during the "real interview." It will also alert you to areas that you need to pay more attention to. Just as an actor never goes on stage "cold" and without advance preparation, you need to practice, practice, practice! At some point, you'll notice that your responses are more easily formulated and you are struggling less with each an-swer. This is the result of interview preparation.

All you need is a mirror to get started. Close the door to your bathroom or bedroom and begin. In front of the mirror, ask your-self a list of typical interview questions and respond to them. Look for nervous mannerisms. Are you fidgeting with your hair, jewelry, or necktie as you answer? Is your voice shaky? Are your responses mumbled or garbled? Stay with each question until you are satisfied with the way you sound and the way you look as you respond.

An ideal way to prepare for interviews is to tape record or videotape yourself. You can then slowly review every aspect of how you responded and remedy any problems with your body language.

All too frequently, beginning job seekers do not do the home-work necessary to present themselves in the best possible way. Don't forget that the first job you get as a result of a successful in-terview may pave the way to an exciting and challenging career.

Once you have made a date for a job interview try to stay fo-cused. Keep the following details in mind:

Time and place

Make sure you know the exact date, time, and place of the interview. Try to get the name and title of the person with whom you will be meeting. If the interviewer's name is unusual, find out how to pronounce it and spell it. Keep these details in a small notepad or pocket diary. Don't rely on your memory, particularly if you are scheduling several interviews at a time. And *never* schedule one interview immediately after another. If you are kept waiting, or if the interview runs longer than you expected, you'll be late for the next one. Allow ample time between each interview, including reasonable travel time from one location to the next. You'll need time to freshen up, have a snack, or just catch your breath. Nothing is more upsetting for a job applicant than dashing into an interview out of breath and apologizing for being late.

Researching companies

Although you may have already done a good deal of research to determine which industries interest you, researching prospective employers is another critical part of your job search. If you don't know much about your target organization, you are at a disadvantage. Larger companies will have annual reports or other descriptive materials available to the public. Work with your school's Placement Office or your college librarian to locate those reports and business clippings that will give you valuable details.

Your librarian will introduce you to a wide variety of excellent sources, including:

- *The Million Dollar Directory*
- *Standard and Poor's Register of Corporations*
- *Standard Directory of Advertisers*
- *Standard Industrial Classification*
- *The Job Seeker's Guide to Private & Public Companies*
- *Moody's Industrial Manual & News Service Report*
- *International Directory of Company Histories*
- *The Reference Book of Corporate Management*

While not many small and mid-sized firms have news clippings about their activities, your career counselor may have information about local businesses and those companies that recruit on your college campus. Alumni who are working in those organizations can also be a good source of information. If the firm you are attempting to research manufactures a product, call the sales office and find out what stores carry that product locally. You can then visit the stores to view the item and familiarize yourself with the price ranges and the lines of competing manufacturers.

Research and Review before Every Interview

Use whatever materials your college placement office has available about specific firms, and use the library to get additional details from directories, industry guides, and newspaper clippings. You should even try to contact the company directly. A receptionist or Human Resources worker can often give you details about products, services, size of the firm, how long it has been in business, a catalog of their products or an annual report.

Aside from gathering information about the company, it is very helpful if you can see the job description for the position you are interested in. If you found out about the job through your college Placement Office, chances are that they will have a copy of the job description. You can go over your qualifications for each of the position's requirements and better prepare for your interview. Write down and say out loud how you think your background, experience, or schooling matches what the employer is seeking. This practice will allow you to shine at the interview. You will be able to provide confident and impressive responses.

For each interview, try to learn:

- What does the company do?
- Does it sell a service, or manufacture or distribute a product?
- Does it perform a service?
- Who are the company's customers?
- Are they consumers?
- Are they other businesses?

- Is it a large or a small operation?
- How many employees?
- How many work locations?

For larger firms or corporations, try to find out:
- Is it a privately or publicly owned firm?
- Is it a local, national, or international business?
- What are the names and the titles of the key executives?
- What are the current issues the firm is dealing with—expansion, competitors, new product lines, or new facilities?

Preparation Leads to Confidence

Every job interview is a chance to be offered a job. You can learn the skills you need to make the most of every interview situation. Good, solid preparation includes thinking about your past accomplishments, your current plans, and your dreams for the future. Preparation allows you to organize information about yourself and present it in the most compelling and positive manner.

To be able to accentuate your **positives**, you must know yourself very well. You need to be able to talk about yourself and where you see yourself heading. But don't show off or brag. You don't want to appear arrogant or pretentious.

Application Forms

Most large firms and many smaller ones have a formal Personnel or Human Resources Department. They will ask you to complete an employment application form. You may even be asked to do so before you meet with the interviewer. Complete the application with a pen, *not* a pencil. Take the time to fill out the form neatly and completely. A messy application form may convince the employer that you are a sloppy worker. Have a notepad with you if you cannot remember all the important dates and facts that you'll need to provide: your social security number, dates of graduation, dates of employment on past jobs or internships, and names of supervisors or references. If a question on the form does not apply to you, simply draw a small line in the space provided for your answer, or write N/A (not applicable). This way it will be clear that you did not simply overlook it.

Application Forms—Summary

- Always complete it in ink. Never use a pencil.
- Print or write as neatly as you can.
- Answer all questions completely. If a question is not relevant to you write N/A in that space.
- Answer all questions honestly and accurately.
- You do not have to give information about your learning disability on an application form.
- Review the form for proper spelling and for accuracy before you turn it in, or ask for another form if you need to re-write it.
- When completing the application form, have the following information with you:
  - Social Security Number
  - Driver's License
  - List of dates, names, and addresses of past jobs or volunteer experiences
  - List of references' names, addresses, and telephone numbers, once you have gotten their permission for you to use them
  - Date of your last medical examination

Dressing for the Interview

How you look is a major part of your overall presentation. *Dress the way you want to be treated!* The clothes you choose and the impression you make will give the interviewer an immediate sense of how businesslike you are. If you look businesslike and professional, it will affect your attitude. You will feel and act businesslike and professional. Your goal in dressing for an interview is to project the image that fits the requirements of the job and the hiring organization. *Always avoid extreme and trendy looks*, unless you are interviewing in the theater or fashion industry.

School is the place for jeans and oversized sweatshirts—not job interviews! You need to look the part—a young worker who could be sent to meet with the firm's clients and key administrators. No employer wants to apologize for an employee's appearance. So don't give interviewers an opportunity to think you may be a potential problem for their firm because of your style of dress.

Your goal is *not* to make a fashion statement or to let the world know what a creative type or non-conformist you are. Your goal is to be taken seriously as a job candidate and land a job offer. So dress appropriately for each interview. When in doubt, conservative dress is best.

Pay attention to the following general guidelines:

- Don't arrive for an interview loaded down with packages or schoolbooks
- Never bring friends or family members with you
- Don't chew gum, smoke, or wear dark glasses

The first impression you make is a lasting one—so make each presentation count. Interviewers can make quick judgments, so use each interview as an opportunity to make a positive impression.

During the Interview

It's hard to imagine getting through an interview without feeling nervous. Most people do get very nervous. Interviews are stressful. But after several interviews, you'll get an idea of what most interviewers expect, and you will feel more at ease. With practice, you'll learn which answers work best for you and in which areas you are not responding as well. Each interviewer's style will vary, and each interview experience that you have will be unique. Some interviewers will greet you warmly and express real interest in you and your background. Others will seem more formal and impersonal. Some interviewers might be talkative and chatty, while others will expect you to take the lead in initiating conversation. Try to prepare for *all* possibilities by planning and practicing in advance of each interview.

- Think about the best answers you can give to commonly asked questions.

- Strengthen your answers by giving specific examples whenever possible.

- Practice talking about your background, your interests and skills, your school experience, and your plans for the future.

- Don't discuss any personal problems or criticize past employers or job situations.

- Be honest in describing your background and qualifications. Employers hiring beginners know they cannot expect extensive work histories.

- Be pleasant, be businesslike.

- Remember to smile as often as you can.

- Above all, try to convey a friendly and positive attitude. This will help put you—and the interviewer—at ease.

While you're concentrating on all these items, you are also working hard during the interview to get information about the job and the firm. It's important to try to listen carefully to the interviewer and express interest and enthusiasm as you respond. If you have a sense that the interview is *not* going well, try not to show your disappointment. After you've left, you can review what may have gone wrong, and learn to avoid those mistakes in future interviews.

Don't take notes during the interview. You can jot down the important details you want to remember immediately afterwards. Try to answer questions fully, without wandering off the topic or rambling on and on. If you are stumped by a tough question, let the interviewer know that you need more time to think about the answer. Afterwards, think through a suitable response to the question, in case that particular question comes up in later interviews.

The Elements of an Interview

In any interview situation, you can usually expect the following steps.

The warm-up

A friendly exchange of greetings and polite conversation will help you relax and break the ice. You can expect to talk about the weather, any travel difficulty in finding the interview location, and other chatty items of this sort.

The interviewer asks questions

If the interviewer is doing his or her job well, you will be encouraged to talk about yourself after the warm-up. The interviewer probably has a planned series of questions. These questions will help him or her determine whether you have the qualifications that the position requires and whether you will fit into the firm.

The interviewer gives information

Another part of the interviewer's job involves selling the position and the company to *you*, by giving you specific details and information about the firm and the industry. This might include a discussion of working conditions and plans for future growth or change. There may also be some mention of salary and the benefits the company provides.

The applicant asks questions

Now is your chance to show that you've done your research. Asking thoughtful questions not already covered in the earlier part of the interview will indicate your interest in the firm and in the job. Always have a group of questions ready to ask.

The wrap-up

This segment of the interview may give you some idea of whether or not you will be considered for the job. You may be told when you can expect to hear about the hiring decision, or be asked to return for a second interview to meet with others in the organization. This is the time for you to thank the interviewer for spending time with you and answering your questions. It's also the right time to re-state your interest in joining the organization—if the job really *does* appeal to you. Try to end each interview on a courteous and positive note.

What the Interviewer Wants to Learn During the Interview:

- Your skill level and your ability to do the job.
- Your short- and long-term career goals.
- Your work values.
- Your personal style and whether you will fit in with the company.
- Any indications of leadership potential or good team spirit.
- Your expectations about salary, advancement, and training opportunities.
- A sense of your commitment to the company.
- Your manner of presentation. Are you friendly, relaxed, at ease, confident?
- Your ability to express yourself clearly.
- How focused you are on a career goal.
- Your interest in the position.
- How well prepared you are. Did you take the time to learn about the firm and the industry?

The more you know and convey to the interviewer, the more impressive a candidate you are!

What You Want to Learn During the Interview:

- Details about specific job duties and responsibilities.

- A broad picture of where you or your department fits into the mission of the firm.
- The title of the person you would be reporting to.
- Why is the job available? Was someone promoted or fired, or is it a new position?
- What skills are necessary to do the job well?
- What are the promotional opportunities?
- Is on-the-job training offered? It is formal or informal?
- How are workers reviewed and evaluated?
- What is the work environment like? Can you walk through the department or the unit?
- Information about salary, company policies, and benefits.

Discrimination

There are laws that protect job seekers from discrimination in a job interview. Title VII of the 1964 Civil Rights Act makes it illegal to discriminate in hiring. The intent of this law is to allow all qualified candidates a chance to apply and compete for all available job openings. It is illegal for interviewers to discriminate against a candidate because of age, religion, race, sex, national origin, marital status, or physical disabilities that do not prevent him or her from doing the job. Most firms make a genuine effort to abide by this law.

The ADA and You

The ADA (Americans with Disabilities Act) of 1990 deals with employers who have 25 or more workers. As of July 1994, employers with 15 or more workers were covered as well. Unless you find a job with a *very* small firm, this legislation will probably cover your work situation. Simply stated, the ADA prohibits job discrimination against people with disabilities. They are protected during the application and interview processes, as well as after a job offer has been made. The protection continues after work has begun.

During the application stage, *an employer may not ask you about the existence of a disability on an employment form.* At the job interview, *an interviewer may not ask about the existence of a disability.* You can *only* be asked if you can perform the essential functions of the job, with or without reasonable accommodations. You may even be asked to demonstrate *how* you would perform the essential functions of that job.

At the hiring stage, *an employer may not deny you a job based solely on the existence of a disability,* or based on the need to provide you with a reasonable accommodation, unless that accommodation is an undue hardship for the employer. Once you are hired, *employers must provide a reasonable accommodation to allow you to perform the job.* They are not required to buy the most expensive accommodation or your choice of accommodation, only what is necessary to do the job. Finally, employers cannot deny a promotion based on a disability or the need for accommodation.

Know Your Legal Rights

If you want to be savvy about your rights, you have to become familiar with the law. You should be aware of what interviewers can legitimately ask you in interviews.

	Acceptable	**Unacceptable**
Age	Can you furnish proof of your age if hired?	How old are you? When were you born?
Education	What schools did you attend? What degrees did you get? What vocational training have you had? Are you currently in school?	What years did you graduate from high school and college?
Religion	No acceptable questions	What is your religion? What religious holidays do you observe?

	Acceptable	**Unacceptable**
		What church are you affiliated with?
Citizenship	Are you a U.S. citizen? Are you legally able to work in the United States?	Are you native born? Are you naturalized? Do you plan to become a citizen?
Nationality	No acceptable questions	What is the nationality of your family?
Language	Do you write or speak fluently in another language?	What language is spoken in your home? What is your native tongue?
Marital Status	No acceptable questions	Are you single, married, divorced?
Arrest Record	How many times were you convicted of a felony? What were you convicted for?	Have you ever been arrested?
Handicapping Condition	Are there any duties relating to the job you're interested in that you cannot perform? Do you have any disability that could prevent you from doing the job?	

If you are not hired, *don't* jump to the conclusion that you were the victim of illegal discrimination. But if you really do feel that you were rejected because of a discriminatory practice, review the situation carefully, as you will have to be sure that you can back up your claim. Even a strongly documented situation against an employer means a great deal of time, effort, and expense. There is never a guarantee of success.

If you do need to register a complaint, discuss *all* the details of the situation with a lawyer representing the local office of the United States Equal Employment Opportunity Commission. You can write to them for information about laws and applicant's rights.

> U.S. Equal Employment Opportunity Commission
> 2401 E. Street, N.W.
> Washington, D.C. 20507

The Issue of Salary

It pays to research current salary ranges. Your college placement and career counselors, professors, and the information available in industry surveys will be resources for you. Even classified ads in newspapers and current department job listings will provide you with up-to-date details about salary trends.

Figure out what you need to survive on by estimating your total monthly expenses. This worksheet will help to give you a general idea, so that you can determine your salary requirements within the going range for a particular position.

Housing

- Rent $ _____
- Gas/electricity   _____
- Telephone   _____

Food

- Groceries   _____
- Eating out   _____

Clothing

- Purchases   _____

- Cleaning/laundry _____

Transportation
- Bus/subway _____
- Travel home _____

Medical
- Doctor/dental _____
- Prescriptions _____

Debts
- Monthly obligations _____
- Credit cards _____

Entertainment
- Movies/videos _____
- Books/magazines _____

Miscellaneous _____

Total _____

Once you have added up all of your anticipated monthly expenses, multiply that figure by 12 to get a yearly figure of what you need to live on—*after taxes*. Don't forget to factor in some extra room for unplanned emergency expenses.

You should not go to an interview without a clear idea of the acceptable salary range for that position. In addition to the dollar amount, be sure that you include other factors in the salary discussion, such as the frequency of salary reviews, the prospect of tuition reimbursement, and benefits that really equate to dollars (such as medical and dental coverage, profit sharing, bonus plans, and stock options).

Always give the interviewer time to raise the salary issue. If the interview is drawing to a close and the job appeals to you—

and there is still no mention of wages—you should feel free to be direct and ask the interviewer what the salary for the position is. It's a good idea to enter into this discussion if you feel reasonably sure that you may be a candidate for the job.

You should also be prepared to be asked, "How much do you think you are worth?" If you've done your research and are familiar with the average range for the job, you can comfortably answer the question without asking for an unreasonable rate or settling on a wage way below the standard. Although there is always room for bargaining and negotiating, beginning workers usually cannot afford to hold out for an exceptionally high salary unless they have unusual credentials or skills. You may be wise to accept a fair salary offer and wait to negotiate for a better salary after your first or second performance review. By that time you will have had your chance to demonstrate your worth on the job.

The starting salary is *not* the most important issue in deciding whether to accept or decline a position. Unless you have great financial need, consider other features before you make your final decision, such as:

- How much learning and training you will receive
- The promotional opportunities that may exist
- A chance to enter the industry or the firm of your choice
- The opportunity to gain experience in a tough job market

Summary: Discussing Your Salary

- Never go to an interview without knowing the typical salary range for the position you are discussing.
- Try not to discuss the issue of salary until you are convinced you are a reasonable candidate for the job. This works best towards the end of the interview.
- When presented with a range, always ask for the high end of the salary.
- Try to let the interviewer state the salary before you indicate the range you're hoping for.

22

Disclosing Your Learning Disability

Should you inform your prospective employers about your learning disability? There is no set answer to this question. The answer could be "maybe," "yes," "sometimes," or "never." You will have to evaluate *each* interview situation and determine whether you feel that disclosure will help or hinder you.

Some people prefer to keep their learning disability a well-hidden secret. They have learned to silently cope with the misunderstanding and lack of clarity that people with learning disabilities often experience. Others are much more open about their limitations as well as their needs. Whether you view your learning disability with distress or accept it as a challenge that must be mastered, you must be clear that your learning problems have nothing to do with being lazy, dull, or slow. And should the situation arise, you may need to convey that to a potential employer. When you are job hunting, the issue of whether or not to disclose information about your learning disability—as well as when and how much information to reveal—can be a major consideration. Give the issue of disclosure the same thought and preparation you would give to any aspect of your job hunt. You want a chance to be viewed as a capable candidate who simply happens to have a learning disability.

The passage of the ADA (Americans with Disabilities Act) made it illegal to discriminate against job applicants with disabilities. Since then, however, people have been puzzled about just how much they should reveal about their limitations in job interviews. Even though you are protected by the ADA, handling the issue of your learning disability can still be awkward and uncomfortable for both you and your interviewer. The hidden nature of a learning disability makes disclosure an unusually tough issue to deal with. Applicants are often perplexed by what to discuss about their particular limitations. What is important to realize, is that *you are always in charge of that decision!* Of course, you should *never* reveal anything you might regret or will be uncomfortable discussing.

It is *your* decision to reveal to others the nature and the degree of your learning problem. Your decision might depend upon the severity of your particular disability. The risk, of course, is that some people may limit your opportunities for success, or even reject you once they learn of your situation, because they do not understand it. Other employers will be more than willing to work with you in emphasizing your strong points and helping to test alternative procedures and coping strategies.

What to Say to Interviewers and Potential Employers

There is no *right* answer for everyone. It depends on how comfortable you are talking about your special needs and explaining what is and what is not a problem for you. Under the law, employers cannot ask if you have a disability. They *can* ask about any special accommodations you would need to do the job. The key is for you to decide *when* and *what* you wish to disclose, and then disclose it in the most positive manner. This may take a bit of practice, but it is really no different than any job applicant attempting to describe a weak area in a positive way. It is important for you to be able to talk about which compensatory strategies work well for you. Do you learn more easily if you have a demonstration, rather than by listening to directions or reading instructions? Make sure you can talk about your own learning style and learning preferences with ease.

Always ask yourself if disclosure of your disability supports your aim of getting hired. You might think of disclosing information about your disability once you have indicated to the interviewer your areas of strength and special skills. You must be specific about your limitations. It will never be helpful for you to declare that you have a learning problem without a brief detail of what the limitation is and how you have learned to deal with it.

Human resources professionals generally welcome a direct statement about your disability, and some discussion about the kind of accommodations you would need, at the time of the interview. This gives you a chance to discuss your particular situation and answer the interviewer's questions. Any earlier mention of your learning disability, such as in a résumé or a cover letter, might allow someone to disqualify you before they have a chance to meet you.

Keep the following statements in mind as you think about how you would discuss your own limitations. Remember that *every* worker has strengths and weaknesses.

- If you are a *slow worker*, you might want to emphasize the fact that you are careful and thorough in your work, even though it may take you a little longer to complete tasks.

- If you have *poor handwriting*, you could talk about the fact that you type your memos and reports or even re-write whatever is illegible.

- If you have *poor math skills*, tell the interviewer that you always use a calculator to ensure that your work is accurate, and that you double-check everything as well.

Discuss your limitations *honestly*. You are the most informed person about what you can do well and what you will need help with. Limit your disclosure to areas that are related to the job you are applying for. For example, if you're interested in a summer job as a gardener's helper where you know you'll be mowing, digging, planting, and the like, your math inadequacy is unrelated and unnecessary to mention.

In many cases, your interviewer may have had very little experience in dealing with people with learning disabilities. He or she may not know a great deal about what accommodation may be suitable. So be patient and polite, while clearly describing any aids or accommodations that will be helpful to you. And be ready to ask your interviewer about job-related expectations.

You are now beginning to take responsibility for your own future. Don't use your disability as a way to limit your own potential or your dreams for the future. Accept the challenge of overcoming the tough spots and work around the areas of your disability. Just as you would not necessarily reveal your learning disability to everyone you meet socially, you will want to be thoughtful about handling disclosure of your learning disability when you are job hunting.

Summary: To Disclose or Not to Disclose

- Disclosure is a *personal* decision and may not be an important issue in every interview. The key question you need to answer is, "Will disclosure of my learning disability at this time help me get hired?"

- Sell yourself at the interview based on your skills and your interest in the job.

- Let employers know about your strong points and accomplishments before discussing your shortcomings. Mention those shortcomings *only* if they will affect your job performance.

- *Never* list your learning disability or areas of weakness on your résumé.

- Do not give those people writing letters of recommendation permission to disclose your learning disability.

- If your disability is *unrelated* to the job you are interviewing for and *you will not need accommodations*, there is no need to disclose it.

23

Job Interview Questions

At most job interviews you will be asked very routine and standard questions. You should practice your responses in advance so that you are ready to answer them. Always listen carefully to each question. Let the interviewer finish asking the question before you jump in to respond. Answer clearly and concisely without rambling on and on, and without exaggerating or bragging.

What You Will Be Asked

Plan on being asked any of the following typical questions.

What interests you about this job?

Here you have the opportunity to describe how you see yourself—your interests, skills, and training—fitting into the organization. You can tell the interviewer what you know about the position and the company. It's a great time to display your enthusiasm for the job and show that you have done your research.

Tell me about your strengths. Why should I hire you?

Here's the chance to discuss your skills and the work-related qualities that the interviewer is looking for: hard-working, reliable, responsible, team player, and so on. Try to connect your strong points to the job you are discussing.

Tell me about yourself.

Although this may sound like an invitation to talk about *anything*, you must stay focused on the fact that this is a job interview. You need to keep your conversation **job-related**. The interviewer wants to hear about your drive, your motivation, your ability to overcome difficult situations successfully, and how well you work with others. Point out all of your strong areas!

What are your weaker areas?

You may not like to discuss these, but sharp interviewers will always pose this question. Be ready to turn any discussion of your limitations into a positive statement.

- "I don't yet have much computer knowledge, but I'd be more than willing to sign up for an evening computer course, or even learn on the job during my lunch hour or after work."
- "My handwriting is not always clear, so I have learned to type all my memos and reports."
- "I have a tough time with numbers and percentages, so I simply keep a pocket calculator with me all the time and use it with ease."

Be honest, but be positive!

What classes did you enjoy most in college?

Here's the opportunity to talk about what you did well in and enjoyed while in school. You might even mention any other courses that you plan to sign up for, either in adult education or graduate programs.

Are there any accomplishments you are particularly proud of?

This is your chance to "toot your own horn" and let the interviewer know more about your successes. Did you raise money for a club on campus? Help organize a drive for the homeless? Plan a dance? Increase membership in an organization? Win an award, learn to play a musical instrument, or teach someone how to play a sport? Perhaps you've gotten your pilot's license? How about just getting through a particularly difficult course, or teaching yourself to speak a foreign language? That's quite a significant accomplishment!

How well do you react under pressure?

Deadlines and time pressures are part of every work situation. This is the time to talk about being organized, how you break jobs down into manageable steps. Don't forget to emphasize teamwork and your willingness to do whatever is needed to get the job done. Interviewers love to have this point confirmed.

What do you feel you can contribute to this company?

Again, it's your chance to itemize and emphasize your best qualities. Stress that you are a committed worker and that you are willing to work hard to get ahead on the job.

Other Typical Questions to Practice Answering

- What have you learned from any part-time jobs or internships?
- How would you describe yourself?
- Talk about your short- and long-term goals.
- Why did you choose this industry? Why are you interested in this firm?
- How do you react to criticism?
- What areas about yourself would you like to improve and develop?
- Where in your career would you like to see yourself in five years? In ten years?

- What are the important rewards you expect from your career?
- What motivates you to put forth your greatest effort?
- How has your college experience prepared you for work?
- What do you think it takes to be successful in the job you're applying for?
- Why did you choose the career you are preparing for?
- What was your most rewarding college experience?
- What have you gained from any of your extracurricular activities?
- In what kind of work environment are you most comfortable?
- What have you learned from your mistakes?

Think About the Tough Questions

Make your own list of questions that you hope you will *not* be asked—then honestly consider how you would respond if you had to. By planning your answer in advance and rehearsing it, you can control the information you share with the interviewer.

Be Ready to Ask Questions

Plan on asking questions that demonstrate your real interest in the company and in the job. Act interested as you ask them. Listen to the answers patiently and attentively. Remember that questions relating to salary, vacation, benefits, and the like are more appropriate to ask at the end of the interview, once it is evident that there is real interest in you as a candidate for the job.

About the firm

- What are the firm's strong points?
- What are the weaker areas? How are they being dealt with?

- What changes in the industry are expected in the near future?
- Who are the major competitors?
- Who are the key clients?
- What long-term strategies are being planned?
- What is being done to respond to new technologies in the field?
- Are there any new products or services on the drawing board?
- Where are the plants and other facilities located?

About the position

- Can you itemize the job's specific duties?
- How are projects assigned?
- Who supervises this position?
- How is the work assessed?
- How much contact is there between the different departments?
- What is a typical career path for a beginner in this position?
- Describe a typical day for someone in this position.
- How does this department relate to the mission of the entire firm?
- What background would the ideal candidate have?

Training

- Is there a formal training program or on-the-job training?
- Are there opportunities to get experience and exposure in other departments?
- Is this position part of a team, or does the person work independently?

Work conditions

- Does the job involve travel? Where? How long? How often?
- What is the philosophy of the organization?
- What is the management style of the head of the firm?
- When will the hiring decision be made?
- How will applicants be informed of the decision?

Never pose questions that ask what the employer or the company can "do for you." You want to impress the interviewer with what *you* are able to offer the organization.

24

Interview Tips

Whenever possible, do a practice run the day before your scheduled interview, especially for the first few interviews. You will discover how long it takes you to travel to the interview site, and you will be able to allow enough time for the actual interview.

Before leaving the house, check your overall presentation. Are your clothes neat, clean, and appropriate for the interview? Choose an interview outfit that fits the business setting. Clothing that is sloppy, too revealing, or too dressy for work will not help you make a good impression. And make sure your fingernails are clean, you are clean-shaven or wearing moderate makeup, and your shoes are shined.

When you meet the interviewer, smile warmly and look him or her in the eye to establish eye contact. Shake the interviewer's hand firmly, but gently, while you introduce yourself. "Hello, Mr. Shimuzu. I'm Roslyn Dolber. It's nice to meet you." Wait until you're invited to sit down before you take a seat.

Keep the conversation upbeat. Stay with positive comments and *never* bad mouth past teachers or employers. Don't volunteer to talk freely about past failures or shortcomings. If an interviewer asks, merely explain the honest circumstances. Don't blame others or give excuses.

Act natural and be yourself. In spite of how nervous or anxious you might feel, your attitude and the manner in which you present yourself will have a strong impact on your interviewer. The interview time is when you are selling yourself!

Have a list of references ready to leave with the interviewer, in case you are asked for them. You *must* check with each person and ask permission before you can use them as a reference in your job search. Never assume that someone is willing to state that you are a reliable or enthusiastic worker until you have spoken with them. For each reference, provide their name, address, telephone number, and job title, if they are a work-related reference.

After the interview, make sure you follow up with any transcripts or other credentials that the interviewer has requested. At the very least, send a handwritten thank-you note thanking the interviewer for meeting with you.

Keep In Mind These Interview Don'ts

- Don't misspell or mispronounce your interviewer's name. Check with the receptionist to be sure you have the right pronunciation.

- Don't argue with the interviewer or show your irritation. Even if you believe the interview is not going well for you, try to remain polite and diplomatic.

- Don't chew gum, smoke, wear dark glasses, or use strong cologne or perfume.

- Don't address the interviewer by his or her first name.

- Don't gaze out of the window or look around the interview room.

- Try to focus on the person talking to you, and make eye contact.

- Don't read the materials or memos on the interviewer's desk.

- Don't apologize if you have little or no past experience. Stress your positives—willingness to learn, loyalty, sense of responsibility, and enthusiasm.

- Don't talk about how many interviews you've already had or how many résumés you've sent out. You do not want to appear as though no one is willing to hire you.

- Don't talk too much or ramble on and on. Take your cues from the interviewer.

- Don't keep glancing at your watch or at a wall or desk clock. It will make the interviewer think you want the interview to end.

- Don't lie about or exaggerate school, work, or volunteer experiences. You must **be honest** in you responses.

- Don't answer questions with trite responses, such as "I just love to work with people," or "I'm seeking a challenging job." *Every entry worker is*!

Certain behaviors are irritating to interviewers. This is behavior that you can concentrate on correcting. Stop yourself from biting your nails, tapping your fingers or feet, and playing with your hair, jewelry, or tie. What about your speech habits? Do you mumble so that it's hard to clearly hear your responses? Do you speak too quickly? In either case, a great answer to an interviewer's question is lost and will never be appreciated. Is your speech filled with unnecessary words and phrases, such as "like," "you know," "ummm"? Pay attention to all these features of your presentation and polish them until you feel comfortable with your interviewing style.

You Can Be an Outstanding Candidate!

As companies strive to operate "lean and mean," more work is delegated to fewer workers. You will need to present yourself as a "can-do" candidate. You must build the best possible case for yourself and let prospective employers know why *you* should be hired. It's okay to say this. It shows your strong interest in, even your passion for, the position. Be genuine and sincere. And be ready to let the interviewer know that you *really* want the job and why. Prepare solid answers to the standard and predictable interview questions, and be ready to respond as best you can to the unexpected inquiries.

- Arrive on time, even a few minutes early.
- Dress appropriately.
- Bring several extra copies of your résumé with you.

- Greet the interviewer by name and with a smile.
- Be ready to answer questions that you have practiced and rehearsed.
- Be prepared to ask the interviewer thoughtful questions that show you have done your research.
- Express enthusiasm and interest.
- Discuss any school or past work achievements as they relate to the job.
- Demonstrate that you have some knowledge of the firm.
- Have good body language. Make eye contact and smile.
- Always be courteous.
- Accentuate your positives. Be confident.
- Don't chew gum or smoke, even if invited to do so.
- Allow the interviewer to lead the conversation.
- Answer questions completely, instead of just saying "yes" or "no." But *don't* ramble on.
- Be yourself and act natural.
- Ask for the job and state why you feel you can handle it.
- Find out when a hiring decision will be made and how you will be informed.
- Thank the interviewer for the opportunity of meeting with her or him.
- Follow up with a brief note of thanks to the interviewer within 48 hours.
- Find out if you are expected to call back to learn of the hiring decision. If so, do it at the proper time.

Immediately After the Interview

After the interview, go over questions you felt you did not answer as well as you would have wanted to. Rethink how you would like to respond so that you'll have a better answer ready the next time you you're asked the same thing. Practice your new answer aloud several times until you are comfortable with it.

Jot down the name and title of the interviewer, as well as the name of any other people you had contact with or were introduced to. Make helpful notes to yourself, including how and when you will be told about a hiring decision.

When you write your thank-you note, restate your real interest in the position. You can re-emphasize any particular skills or background that relate to the job. Of course, thank the interviewer for the time spent with you and mention the names of others who may have met with you during the interview.

Interview Checklist

Review these items after each interview to determine what you need to improve for the next interview.

Presentation

- Did you arrive on time?
- Was your body language appropriate?
- Did you return the interviewer's greeting, introduce yourself, and establish eye contact?

Objectives

- Were you able to clearly state why you want the job?
- Did you discuss your immediate and long-term goals?

Background

- Did you describe relevant work or school experience?
- Did you mention related skills, strengths, and interests?

Research

- Did you convey information you learned about the industry, the firm, or the specific job?

Closing

- Did you express genuine enthusiasm?
- Did you thank the interviewer and establish what the next step will be for you?

What to Expect

Don't be surprised if you are asked to return for more than one interview. It is a sign that you are still in the running. You may even be asked to meet with several people during the course of a single interview, either in a group or one at a time. This is a fairly common practice. Employers want to be sure that they are selecting the best applicant. It is too expensive for them to hire and train workers who are a poor fit for the position or for their organization.

Every applicant, no matter how strong, must be prepared for rejection. The job hunting process always involves being turned down by prospective employers—*often more than once!* This does not mean that you are not a fine candidate. It simply means that your skills and background are not what the company is seeking at that time.

Interview Summary

If you aren't prepared for *each* interview you are wasting your time!

Know yourself

Be able to discuss with ease your:

- skills
- interests
- school background
- any special training
- related hobbies

- personal qualities
- limitations and how you work around them
- your immediate and long-term goals

Do your research for every interview

- Learn what you can about the industry, the company, and the specific job.

Take every interview seriously

- Be prepared for every interview.
- Arrive on time; early is best.
- Have extra résumé copies.
- Practice clear responses to typical questions.
- Have questions for the interviewer prepared.
- Be familiar with salary ranges for the position.
- Know how to respond to job offers.
- Dress appropriately—first impressions are lasting ones.
- Maintain good posture and eye contact.
- Get permission from people you'd like to use as references.
- Show real interest in each interview; be enthusiastic.
- Indicate you are eager, rather than resistant, to learn on the job.
- If you can give concrete examples of being reliable, responsible, a team player, etc, do so.
- Discuss salary and benefits only if you feel you are a serious candidate.
- Thank the interviewer at the close of the interview.
- Send a thank-you note within 48 hours.
- Make a note of anything further you need to do, such as call back on a particular date to find out if you were hired.

Thank-You Notes

Within 48 hours of every job interview, remember to send a thank-you note to each interviewer. These notes are professional business letters and are different from the typical thank-you note you might casually send to a friend or relative.

In addition to routinely sending notes of thanks to all who interviewed you, don't overlook contacts who gave you job leads or advice while you were searching. The thoughtfulness will be appreciated, even by those people you use as references. Most will be delighted to hear about the progress of your job hunt and will remember your courteous gesture.

The standard thank-you note after a job interview should:

- Remind the interviewer of who you are and which job you interviewed for

- Restate why you are qualified for the position and cover any areas you may have missed in the interview

- Let the interviewer know that you are very interested in the job

Even if you are not interested in the particular job that was discussed at the interview, write a note of thanks. Interviewers appreciate the gesture, and will remember you when they make their hiring decisions.

Design your note so that you get the points itemized above in just two or three short paragraphs. Then mail it *immediately*. It will be of little value if it arrives at its destination days or weeks after your interview. Make your message sound like you and try to personalize it and relate it to your specific interview experience. Just as with your cover letter and résumé, it must sound good, look good and be error-free.

Use these brief thank-you notes to help keep the doors open—you may want to be in touch with these contacts later in your career or in future job searches.

Sample Thank-You Note

today's date

Carla Hightower
Bryce Publishers
550 North Broadway
Washington, DC 20201

Dear Ms. Hightower:

Thank you for meeting with me on February 25th to discuss my interest in joining Bryce's training program.

As I stated in the interview, I have just completed the journalism program at Emory University. I am eager to apply my related school background and the work experience I gained at Gannett Publications to your training program, which could lead to a junior copywriting position.

I believe my skills and enthusiasm will allow me to be a productive member of your organization. As we agreed at our meeting, I will call you on March 1st to hear your hiring decision.

Sincerely,

sign your name
type your name

25

Job-Seeking Strategies in a Tough Market

It can take a lot of effort to land the right job. In the meantime, you need to keep your spirits up, and take it one step at a time. You need to stay focused—and you need to keep busy!

- Always carry a supply of résumés with you and give them to anyone who might be helpful in your job search.

- Keep networking. Just *one* lead or contact may be the key for you.

- Register with your college's Career Placement Office.

- Use all available resources. Don't ignore the obvious: teachers, friends, family members, alumni association, OCR recruitment programs, classified ads in newspapers, professional and trade meetings, professional journals, public and private employment agencies (avoid those that charge you a fee)—even the telephone directory, which lists employers by specific industries.

- Consider **temping** to tide you over. A temporary assignment can give you current work experience, exposure to various fields of work, and access to many new contacts. A temporary job can even turn into a career opportunity. Nearly 40 percent of all temp workers are offered full-time jobs, according to a nationwide study.

- Always be businesslike. Treat a temp or part-time job as seriously as any other. Good recommendations go a long way.

- Look the part. Whether dressing for an interview or just picking up an employment application, your appearance counts.

- Be persistent and assertive. Follow up regularly with every lead and every contact.

- Be positive. Your attitude comes across in everything you do.

- Be helpful to others who are job hunting. And once hired, share the information, leads, and suggestions that were valuable to you.

- Be realistic. Concentrate on following up on one lead or contact at a time, and *make the most of it*.

- Keep up-to-date. Read the newspaper every day and keep up with business magazines and professional journals. That way you will always be current and aware of what's happening in the industry you are trying to enter.

- Keep organized. Keep accurate notes of firms you've interviewed with, people you've sent thank-you notes to, dates that you need to call interviewers back, and so on. Although these little details are often a chore, they are important if you want to stay on top of the job search.

- Stay motivated. Finding a job, particularly an entry-level position, takes energy and effort. The one contact that you need to make things happen will come along, if you keep searching. Don't give up!

Keeping Your Options Open

The job market is always changing. In many industries—and in many regions of the country—you might face tough competition as you search for an entry-level job. Here are some tips to consider in a tight job market. You'll need to work hard and be flexible.

Always have a fallback plan

Your first choice of job may not always be available to you when you are ready for it. If you have other interests to fall back on, you won't feel quite as discouraged while you wait for your initial option to come about. Consider and prepare for more than one career choice.

Network, network, network

More than half of all job seekers find the right lead as a result of this wonderful process of building contacts. In fact, you should get so used to relying on this source of information that you continue to network even after you have gotten a job.

Be flexible

Consider *any* job in a firm or field of work that interests you, even if it's not the job you originally hoped for. Once hired, you can learn about the politics and culture of the organization and find ways to move on to a more desirable level.

Consider temping

Using a temporary employment service will not only keep the salary coming in, but will help you learn more about various career paths. You may even link up with an employer who can keep you on for a while. More and more industries hire temps to get them through busy or seasonal periods. And sometimes these temporary jobs are converted into full-time positions.

Consider volunteering

If you truly want to break into a particular company or field of work and just cannot get a foot in the door, investigate volunteer opportunities. If you give it your best shot, you may be a strong consideration when hiring starts up. This is particularly true for community service and social agencies, which rely heavily on volunteers. Strive to make yourself indispensable!

Go on informational interviews

Be the best informed job applicant possible by arranging meetings with people working in fields that appeal to you. Be sure to ask about hiring trends in that field, what you can do to become a stronger candidate, and suggestions for additional contacts.

Never, *never* ask your contacts for job leads. The purpose of your visit is *strictly* to gather information

Go to school

Use your free time to upgrade your marketable skills. Get advanced training or degrees, if they will make a difference in how employers view you as a candidate. Diverse skills may give you the hiring edge that you need. At the very least, be computer literate. Sign up for classes in word processing, accounting, and database programs if you are not already familiar with them.

Talk to experts

Don't lose touch with the professionals who can help you. You need support and encouragement as much as you need actual job leads. Go over your employment situation with your college career counselor periodically to keep her or him updated on your progress and to check out new leads.

Consider a new location

Feeling brave? Think about identifying several cities where job opportunities may be more numerous than in your locale. Remember that the job market is not the same all over. Be sure you do plenty of research in advance of any move. Check out the region, housing and salary ranges, weather patterns, availability of public transportation, as well as specific employers and trade or industry associations. You can learn a great deal by subscribing to out-of-state newspapers and reviewing their classified ads, or reading the papers at your local library.

Be critical of your résumé and cover letter

Dozens of applicants are likely to apply for the same positions that interest you. Aim to make your cover letter and résumé stand out! Have them reviewed by a career counselor or human resources professional. Sit in on as many job skills workshops as you can. Always review your current résumé to make sure it has been updated and makes you look your best!

26

Evaluating Job Offers

No one can tell you which job offer is really the best one for you. Only *you* have the knowledge and power to determine what will be most important for you in a work setting. You have to imagine what it would be like going to work each day at the firm that has made you an offer. How will you feel about your duties, your co-workers, the physical work environment, and the training and promotional policies of the firm? Do you believe you will feel capable of and comfortable in performing your duties? Will you be challenged so that you grow on the job?

Knowing What Matters to You

When evaluating job offers, you need to consider positions that are compatible with your values, interests, and skills. Accepting an offer is quite a big step. It represents a commitment, and may play an important role in your career and your future. It's wise to consider *all* of your options before you reject or accept an offer. This means completing all interviews on your schedule if you feel you will miss out on an outstanding opportunity.

An interviewer might offer you a job on your first or second interview with that firm. This is a difficult moment, as it's much easier to have an offer presented to you by mail or phone, when you are not in the midst of the interview situation and you've had the time to mull it over or even discuss it with family, friends, or professors. There are several guidelines that you can keep in mind to help you make the right decision.

What's really important in your first job, or in beginning jobs, is the potential it may hold for the future. Often, it is hard to recognize. Deciding which job offer to accept is both difficult and exciting, because you never know where it will lead. What happens early on may determine your path for the future. When hiring entry-level employees, many firms are interested in a person who will grow with the company. And, of course, you are interested in finding a company where you will learn and advance.

Factors to Consider

The immediate issues—type of work, salary, and location—that are a concrete part of a job offer tend to be the ones that are easier to accept or reject. The long-range factors—quality of supervision, opportunity for growth, professional development, management style, and company culture—are harder to evaluate until you are on the job. These long-range factors, however, may be critical in determining if you will be satisfied with your choice of job or organization.

Review the following immediate and long-range factors, along with the recommendations for allowing you to assess each issue.

Opportunity for Growth

The **type of work** you will be involved in will influence your selection of a job. The tasks should match your skills and training, and the projects should be challenging for you. Your job interviews should leave you with a good sense of the type and level of work you will be expected to do. However, what you might do in the future is usually not as clear, even though future opportunities are vital to long-term satisfaction.

There are several questions you can ask to try to evaluate future opportunities:

- What might I expect to be responsible for or working on within the next three to five years? What assignments or added responsibilities might I be given?

- What would a typical career path be for someone hired into the position we are discussing? What are the promotional possibilities?
- Are lateral or rotational moves provided to allow for broad exposure? Does the organization value this? Is it expected or preferred?

Training and Continuing Education

The training you receive, whether formal classroom training or more informal on-the-job training, will allow you to develop the skills you need to succeed. Your interview questions should provide you with information on the amount and the extent of the training you will be getting and how organized or informal it will be. Although training is very important for your first position, ongoing education is very important for your long-term development. Continuing education is really ongoing training, which keeps you current with the trends and new developments in any field.

Every industry is experiencing great changes and movement as we head toward the 21st century.

In some technical areas, the skills you have mastered in college may quickly become outdated. It will be up to *you* to keep pace with the rapid growth that is happening all around us.

Some employers support continuing education programs for workers by offering company courses and professional seminars. Others even sponsor tuition reimbursement for university-level coursework. Learn whatever you can about a firm's employee development programs.

- Is any training offered to workers?
- Are employees able to take advantage of any continuing education programs in local colleges and universities?
- Are employees encouraged to do so?
- How do you help employees stay up-to-date on changes and new developments in the field?

Supervision and Quality of Management

Your feelings about the person who would be your supervisor will probably account for a large part of your decision to accept or reject any job offer. You will want to look for a supervisor who indicates interest in your growth as a professional. You need to feel comfortable about that individual's manner of relating to you.

If your direct supervisor was part of the interview process, you probably got a fair idea of his or her interpersonal style. Nevertheless, work situations often result in unforeseen changes within departments and divisions, so the overall style of management is perhaps a more important issue for you. Quality of management offers a broad basis for how successful the business—as well as the employees—are managed.

Ask questions that will help you get a picture of the company's management philosophy.

- What is the firm's view of managing the business and the employees?

- What are the strengths of the company's management?

- How does an employee become a supervisor or a manager in the firm?

- Does the firm encourage the practice of promoting managers from within?

Work Environment/Company Values

Naturally, you will want to select a work environment in which you feel comfortable and at ease, based on your own work style. Whether you prefer a formal or casual, rural or urban, or elegant or simple work setting is a very subjective decision. You may already know what is comfortable for you, or you will learn quickly. Remember, the work environment generally reflects the organization's value system. Lack of status symbols—for everyone from the boss to the mail room crew—may indicate a "we're all equal" philosophy, rather than an elitist one. This sort of atmosphere will appeal to some people. Company values are often very important in long-term satisfaction, as those values tend to have great impact on many parts of the firm's operations. It's very helpful if you can uncover those organizational values to see how closely they mesh with your own.

- What does the company stand for? What are its values?

- How are they reflected in everyday activities?

- What is the work environment? Structured or unstructured? Casual or formal?

- What types of workers are most successful at the firm? What qualities are valued?

Salary and Compensation

A dramatically high or low salary will certainly influence your decision on whether to accept or reject a job offer. Make an effort to learn about the company's compensation policies. Ask about the system for job and performance reviews, and determine your potential for both salary and career growth. Try to learn on what basis raises are given. Is it for performance, length of service, or other factors? *The bottom line is your earning potential and how it is assessed.* This is more important than your starting salary.

- What is the salary scale for the first few years for this job title?

- How are raises determined?

- Have any recent changes been made to the benefits package to keep it current and competitive?

> The job you decide to accept should be based on long-range as well as immediate and more concrete factors. It's your first step toward your goal!

Evaluating a Job Offer

These guidelines can help you weigh the merits of a position you are offered.

Company Name _____ **Position Offered** _____
Skills/Abilities
List the skills/abilities you will **use** on this job:_____
_____
List the skills/abilities you can **develop** on this job:_____
_____

Work Values
List the work values you feel **will be met** on this job:_____
_____

List the work values you feel **will not be met** on this job:_____
_____

Personal Qualities
List the personal qualities you will **use** on this job:_____
_____

List the personal qualities you feel you can **develop** on this job:
_____

Development/Training
Will the training be formal or informal? _____
Who will be your immediate supervisor? _____
Do you feel comfortable about working with her/him as a supervisor and mentor? _____

Environment
Do the physical surroundings, co-workers you have met, location, and other factors make you think you will enjoy working for this firm? _____

Is the location reasonably accessible to you, so that extensive daily travel is not an issue? _____

If job-related travel is required, will you be able to do it? _____

Salary/Benefits
What is your starting salary? _____
When is your first salary review? _____
Is this salary within the range you were seeking? _____
Is it acceptable? _____

Lifestyle
In considering all of the factors mentioned above, how will this position enhance or detract from the lifestyle you wish to lead?
_____

What will you learn from this job? _____
_____

Do you believe the firm will offer you room for career advancement? _____

You should accept this position, because:_____
_____

You should not accept the offer, because:_____
_____

If you feel **sure** that this is the job you want and you do not want to have further interviews at other firms, accept the offer courteously with a definite "yes." Find out the exact date, time, and place you should show up for work. Get the name of the person to whom you will report, and make sure you know which department or division you have been hired for.

Make sure you are clear about your starting salary. It is appropriate to double-check whatever financial arrangement has been discussed. *Never* accept a position without being very sure of this issue. Larger organizations may routinely send you a letter specifying all the terms of your new employment, including your salary and other benefits. At many small firms, where personnel procedures are conducted in an informal manner, you may receive only a verbal commitment. You can suggest that it be put in writing, but it is not always standard operating procedure.

At this point you might also be asked to fill out standard forms for the payroll unit. This may be done on your first day on the job. Of course, once you accept a job offer, you must courteously cancel all scheduled interviews with other companies. Simply let them know that you are no longer available. It is considered unethical to continue interviewing once you have accepted a job. You would not expect your new employer to continue interviewing other candidates, and similarly, you must also end your job search.

In some case *you* may be asked to submit a formal letter of acceptance. The following example can be used as a model.

Date
Roslyn Dolber, Personnel Director
XYZ Corporation
11 Gables Way
Boca Raton, FL 34617

Dear Ms. Dolber,

I am delighted to accept the position of editorial assistant.

As we discussed in the interview, I will begin work on _____.

I will report to Ernesto Cruz at 9:00 AM at the South Street office. The starting salary of $20,500 per year is acceptable to me, as well.

I believe I can make a significant contribution to the XYZ Corporation and I look forward to joining your staff.

Yours truly,

(signature)
Matthew Philip

Declining a Job Offer

If you are *not* ready to accept an offer, let the interviewer know that you'd like to review the offer and call back with your decision. You may have doubts about some aspects of the job and be unsure of how suitable it is for you. Or you may just need to talk it over with family or friends. Make sure that you let the interviewer know how much you appreciate the offer, and make a note to yourself of when you agreed to call back with your decision. Try to reach your decision within two to four days. And be sure that you do call back when you agreed to, regardless of your decision. It is a courtesy that the spot is being held for you!

If you want to decline a job offer, it is important that you express your thanks for the offer and for the interviewer's interest in you. You may want to consider that same firm at a later time, so be as professional as you can. You might even want to mention the reason that you are rejecting the job offer, so that the interviewer will understand. For example, you might say: "As you described the position I realized that I would not have the chance to learn your computerized systems, and I'm quite interested in that particular area. But I do want to thank you for offering me the opportunity."

If you find that it's easier for you to write a letter declining the offer than discussing it on the telephone, do so. The following sample letter can be used as a guide.

Date
Roslyn Dolber, Personnel Director
XYZ Corporation
11 Gables Way
Boca Raton, FL 34617

Dear Ms. Dolber,

Thank you for your job offer to begin work as an editorial assistant. I have given much thought to the job description and have decided to decline your offer.

I realize that I would not have the opportunity to learn your computerized systems. As I stressed in my interview with you, this is an area of great interest to me.

I appreciate your willingness to have me join your company and I hope that I have a future opportunity to be a consideration at the XYZ Corporation.

Yours truly,

(signature)
Matthew Philip

Requesting a Delay

You may have other job opportunities to explore when a job offer is presented to you. Don't panic! Try to salvage the situation by politely requesting some additional time. Be diplomatic, but honest, in stating that you have several other interview commitments scheduled that you'd like to honor, or that you want to take additional time to review the job offer in greater detail. *This may not always work*. Interviewers don't like to hear about other organizations you are interested in or that you are not jumping to accept their job offer. But more sophisticated interviewers realize that the best applicant they can hire is one who *truly* wants to be a part of their organization. They will usually extend a reasonable amount of time for you to make your decision.

If you are lucky and get a time extension, make a note of the date you are expected to get back with your decision—and honor it! Be gracious and show your appreciation for this courtesy. *Always get back to the interviewer by the date agreed upon.*

Why Applicants Are Rejected

Employers frequently complain about entry-level job seekers. They often feel that applicants:

- Are unaware of the realities of the industry, and have unrealistic work and promotion expectations
- Have poor attitudes and seem to believe that the employer "owes them something"
- Have weak communication skills
- Have weak math and problem-solving abilities

Employers would like to see entry-level applicants:

- Who have some related work experience
- With good speaking and writing skills
- Who demonstrate leadership qualities
- Who can work as part of a team
- Who can accept constructive criticism
- Who acknowledge their mistakes without excuses or blaming others
- Who complete projects when they are due and can meet deadlines
- Who can clearly convey their ideas
- Who can communicate well—both orally and in writing
- Who listen carefully and follow directions
- Who ask questions if they are unsure

Interviewers and employers try hard to make the right hiring decisions. It's their *job* to try to hire the person they feel is best suited for each assignment. Naturally, they will react poorly to a poor attitude or sloppy appearance. These are some of the top reasons they reject job candidates:

- Lack of enthusiasm
- Arriving late for the interview
- Body language that includes poor posture, no eye contact with the interviewer, not smiling or seeming tense
- Unbusinesslike appearance
- Inability to answer interview questions
- Overemphasis on salary, vacation, and benefits
- Discourteous, arrogant manner
- No expression of interest in the job or the firm
- No knowledge about the company, the product, or the service
- No sense of flexibility or willingness to pitch in to do the job
- Unable to discuss skills, strengths, and background
- Badmouthing past employers or professors at school

Never stop your job search until you have had a job offer and you have accepted it. You must not assume that having a good interview with a friendly recruiter means that you are the firm's top candidate. Circumstances change rapidly. You may in fact have been an interviewer's first choice until the next applicant appeared. Or until the boss's kid decided to look for work. Stay with your job hunt until you and the interviewer have agreed on a definite commitment and start date.

27

Your First Job

It's never just a matter of being in the right place at the right time. Success on the job must be *learned* and *earned*. It will take planning on your part, and hard work as well. Success is rarely a matter of luck alone.

Making the Transition from Student to Employee

As you begin your new job, first impressions are very important. You are walking into a new group of co-workers, supervisors, and administrators. And you want to come across as hard-working and productive. In other words, as the *right* person for that job. This can be a tough adjustment. You are in an unfamiliar setting, where you are about to spend eight or more hours every workday. How you handle yourself during your first few weeks on the new job may be very telling to others. You will probably be feeling some stress. The *most* important issue for you is to do your job well. Your good work and efforts to learn will be welcomed and remembered. Make a commitment to do the very best job that you can, in the most professional manner. Take a real interest in the company you're working for and demonstrate that interest through your attitude. Show enthusiasm for the work, service, or product—and contribute to making it better!

Your first full-time position may set the stage for a series of advancements or opportunities. How you work and behave now could color your future dramatically. This is *the* time for you to develop and perfect your work skills. You can test out and improve your interpersonal and communication skills. And you can use this opportunity to try to address your weak spots.

Make the most of this new job opportunity. Chances are your employer will be interested in seeing that you are productive and that you handle your responsibilities. There are several ways you may be trained on your new job.

On-the-job training.   This involves simply doing your regular job duties under the supervision of more senior colleagues, as well as working with your direct supervisor.

Rotational training programs.   These programs provide training in different parts of the company and are generally scheduled for the short term, usually several weeks or months. You should expect your progress to be evaluated at the end of each rotation.

Classroom training.   This more formal approach is often integrated along with on-the-job training or rotational training programs, to enhance and supplement your progress. The classroom portion is actually like a real "classroom" situation. Speakers give lectures and you are expected to participate in group discussions.

The sink-or-swim method.   Unfortunately, some less-sophisticated firms resort to this approach. You are left on your own with only vague information or instructions about how to function in your job. You need to be **assertive** in asking for clarification of your duties and for feedback as to how well you are performing.

In all cases, take the initiative. Let your supervisor know your interests. You do not have to wait for an annual employee evaluation. Take advantage of every opportunity to learn more and more. Stay informed about any opportunities that interest you within the firm, and look for ways to get involved in special projects or assignments. This will serve to enhance your value to the company!

Gain what you can from this first job and it will serve you well as you move on to more challenging assignments. Don't spend too much time at work talking about the good old days in college.

It's time to shed your student image and develop a real professional identity. So use your first weeks and months in the new work setting to observe and learn as much as you can.

Be Ready to Work Hard

Regardless of your brand new title, you are the *low* person on the office totem pole. You will be expected to pitch in and apply yourself from the minute you step into the job. It is really true that beginners are observed and evaluated more often than senior workers, so be ready for lots of people paying close attention to the kind of job you're doing.

Learn by Listening and Observing

Make it your business to find out about everything that goes on in your unit, department, or division. The *first* mandate, however, is to do your *own* job well. After that, try to see the big picture—how the smaller pieces all fit into the larger scheme of things. Learn about other jobs both inside and outside of your unit. Don't limit yourself to being concerned with just your particular set of responsibilities. At some point, you could be familiar with every operation you or your department has contact with. Imagine how valuable an employee this makes you! You can easily pick up tips and information about other functions and how other departments are organized.

Learn about new developments within the firm, or plans for expansion. Find out about the problem areas that the firm is struggling with. Observe how other workers handle their responsibilities. You will learn the ropes more quickly, and your supervisor is likely to appreciate your interest and eagerness to get to know the larger picture of the operation.

You can gather a lot of information just by listening to the people you work with. People really appreciate being listened to. And you don't even have to venture an opinion or take a stand on an issue. Just by listening, you will learn a lot about the organization and what areas may best use your talents in the future. You might even have some ideas that are worth sharing with the boss. At the very least, you will be informed and aware of the work environment around you.

Uncover the Unwritten Rules

Every firm, and every individual department or division, has a "culture" or set of unwritten rules by which they operate. Usually no one even takes the time to explain these guidelines to new employees, but you'll certainly be expected to adhere to them. You can pick up on these standards of behavior by keeping your eyes and ears open, or ask a co-worker about the specifics you feel you need to know. For example, if everyone returns promptly from their one-hour lunch break, you must do the same. If your colleagues drift in and out of the office in a casual way, without paying strict attention to the clock, you can take your cue from that observation or check with your supervisor to be sure that you understand the company policy. It may be that workers who take a leisurely lunch break come in earlier or leave later to complete their assignments. You need to know this!

It will take you a bit of time to discover how people are expected to operate, but for starters, use your own good judgment. Do not take liberties with the more traditional workplace expectations. Show up for work promptly and maintain a good attendance record. Unlike college, there is no such thing as "cutting" work. You are paid to show up and do your job, unless you are ill.

Ask Questions

Don't be embarrassed or timid when you are unsure what you should do next or unclear how to finish a routine that you've begun, even if it has been explained to you before. Your supervisor would prefer that you stop and get the correct information before you proceed. However, it probably won't be necessary to stop your boss *every* time a question comes to mind. Jot down those items that you feel need additional discussion or clarification. Then find some time when your boss has the freedom to go over them with you. If you are truly stumped and cannot go on with your assignment, check with a knowledgeable co-worker, or get your boss's attention, so that you can proceed with your work.

Don't forget that your experienced co-workers can be a great source of guidance and information for you, particularly if you need help with simple routines and basic procedures. But you should always check with your direct supervisor when you need guidelines for specific projects.

Take It All Down

In the beginning you will probably be bombarded with facts, figures, new routines, and new names and faces. There will also be new procedures that you will be expected to follow. Try to jot down any information that you might need to refer to. Keep a notebook or folder at your desk or workstation so you can write new information down immediately. It will help you in many ways, from being able to quickly retrieve the name of the president's secretary to not having to bother your boss or supervisor for information.

What's On First?

An organized supervisor will surely let you know what tasks need your immediate attention. We're not all lucky enough to have a supervisor who will help us establish priorities. As a new worker, there is really no way for you to know what jobs need to be done promptly and what jobs do not require immediate attention. Once you get a clearer idea of the mission of your department or your boss's priorities, you will know how to schedule your own workload. Until then, ask for specific instructions about what you are expected to tackle first. You might ask this at the start of each week, or even daily if things change rapidly in your department.

Have a Short-Term Goal

Identify a specific, measurable, and achievable goal within the framework of your job. Many people work for the income and security that the job brings. Other people concentrate on using their first job as a stepping-stone up the career ladder. Set your sights on a target that makes sense for your career plans, whether they involve working with computers to gain greater facility, having reservation experience to learn about front-office hotel operations, or whatever suits your own goals. After about a year in your entry-level job, you can assess how close you are to meeting your goal. Are you really spending as much time working on the computer as you thought you would? Do you need to arrange with your boss so that you have more time to do so?

Improve Yourself

You already have a good sense of your own strengths and weaknesses. Now you have a chance to improve those areas that need work. You might identify some of the skills you observe in some of your more successful colleagues. Do the more advanced workers have some knowledge or expertise that you might pick up on the job? Would you consider taking an evening course to acquire that skill? Will your firm offer a tuition refund?

Have you just begun to learn something that might ultimately prove beneficial to your department? If you become expert in desktop publishing, would your boss value that? If you learned to master a particular piece of machinery or equipment, would you be more valuable to your department?

Think about self-improvement in terms of your own interests as well as what it will mean to your company.

Be Flexible

Be cooperative. Assist your colleagues whenever you are able to do so without interrupting your own work routines. You will certainly need their assistance at some point and if you help them you can more freely ask for *their* help. It's fine to become known as a co-worker who is always ready to pitch in and go the extra mile when it's needed.

Be Upbeat

Take a real interest in the organization and the job you were hired to do, and show it! Your enthusiasm will be noted.

Find a Mentor

Try to seek out a seasoned worker or even a supervisor who recognizes your talents and your interest in the company. Your mentor can act as your guide, teaching you the ropes or serving as your advocate. A mentor can help clue you in on the company's unwritten rules of the road. A mentor is often very helpful in fostering your growth. He or she can give you interesting or unusual assignments that will stretch your abilities, or your mentor can allow you to take credit for doing challenging work. Mentor relationships are especially valuable in larger, more impersonal organizations.

You don't need to rely on a single person to fill the traditional mentor role. Many younger workers cultivate several mentors who can offer advice and guide them on a variety of issues. You can learn different things from different people, whether they hold positions above or below you in the firm. Lower-level co-workers may be great resources for technical tips or advice on how to handle a difficult supervisor.

You might want to think in terms of developing a group of people to whom you can turn for guidance, direction, and support. Look for people whose work you respect or who have skills and abilities quite different from your own. Someone with a different perspective will help you see the broad picture of the company.

Mistakes Will Happen

Yes, they really do happen to everyone. No one is immune. You need to learn to acknowledge your errors and profit from them by knowing what to avoid or to do better the next time. No one will demand perfection on the job all the time, particularly not in the early stages of your career. And if you believe that everything you do must be perfect, you will *always* fall short of the mark and be frustrated and disappointed with your work performance. Even seasoned professionals make errors, so you need to learn to live with them and move forward. Admit your errors and you will gain the respect of those you work with.

Take One Step at a Time

You cannot dash up the career ladder all at once! Beginners often lose sight of the fact that it is so easy to stumble and fall unless you take it a step at a time. A good way to develop patience is to set goals that are appropriate. You know you won't be moved from an entry-level spot to the president's seat in the near future, so why not put that plan on the back burner for a while and concentrate on what is realistic and attainable? Think in terms of two-year blocks of time. Where would you like to see yourself in the company two years from now? This is a specific goal and will give you ample time to refine or acquire the skills you need to compete for such a job. Once that is mastered, on to the next step!

Show That You Are a Professional

It's unlikely that your first position will last a lifetime. But for as long as it does last, make it work for you by realizing that you can grow and learn in *every* situation. It will probably take four to six months before you truly feel at ease and relaxed on the job. It takes that much time to learn about and absorb the new work and organizational routines, and get to know the many different people you may be dealing with. It also takes several months to sort out the more subtle, unwritten rules of the company's culture. So don't expect things to fall into place quickly or easily.

Smaller Firms

In a smaller company you will have the opportunity to wear many hats. You will get to try your hand at a variety of different functions, often filling in for or backing up other employees. This is a great chance to find out about areas in other departments that you really enjoy, or to identify skills and areas of expertise that you'd like to explore.

In a small and more intimate work setting, it is often easier to see the impact your work has on the product or the level of service. That can be very gratifying.

Small, lean firms truly can't afford to have non-productive workers, so you'll be expected to carry your own weight and pitch in and help others when needed. This is often rewarded by having a supervisor or boss who is more aware of how cooperative you are. They have more opportunities to see your willingness to work towards getting the job done.

How Good Are Your Work Habits?

There are a number of critical areas that beginning workers need to be particularly sensitive to. Could you use improvement in any of these?

Attendance

Your boss needs to be able to count on you to show up at work each day that you are scheduled. Other workers, as well as clients, may also be counting on you. When you are not able to report for work, you must have a solid reason. Be sure to let your employer know *as early as possible*.

Punctuality

Your supervisor and co-workers will depend on you to show up on time and be ready to begin your assignment each day. If you will be reporting to work late, you'll need to call your employer to alert her or him.

Team Player

People who work together count on each other. They rely on co-workers for cooperation and flexibility. Employees need to treat each other with respect and courtesy and be considerate of their feelings. Many workers have difficulty dealing with colleagues because they have never learned to cooperate with others.

Criticism

You must be ready to hear criticism about your performance at work. Most likely it is meant to help you do a better job. You'll need to take this kind of criticism without becoming defensive or angry. Try to profit from the feedback of supervisors or other more experienced workers.

Summary: Survival Tips for Your First Job

- Be ready to work hard.
- Learn by listening and observing.

- Uncover the company culture.
- Ask questions.
- Jot it all down.
- Establish priorities.
- Set your own short-term goals.
- Keep improving your skills.
- Be flexible.
- Show your enthusiasm.
- Find a mentor, or several mentors.
- Learn from your mistakes.
- Take one step at a time.
- Always be professional.

Remember that your job success and your job security ultimately come from taking charge of your career and demonstrating that you are a valuable employee. Work hard to become one!

28

On the New Job

Few beginning workers realize that it takes some time to understand the responsibilities and obligations of becoming a full-fledged worker. In this unusual transition stage, you are no longer a student—but you are not really a professional just yet either.

What to Expect in the Beginning

You are the low man or woman on the totem pole, and each co-worker will respond to you and judge you differently. Entry-level workers need to learn a new set of rules so they can get a jump start on their career.

Realistic expectations and appropriate attitudes are essential. You will need to learn how things are done in the new organization. The manner in which you approach your supervisor and your co-workers will have great impact on your success. Many early career opportunities become available to workers based on the early impressions they make on their new job.

Use the early stages of your beginning employment to establish yourself as a capable and responsible worker, worthy of the respect of your co-workers. Once this is established, you will more than likely be offered the opportunity to become more visible to upper management and make more of a contribution to the organization. *Demonstrate that you are a serious worker*. Opportunities to display your abilities will follow. If you appear arrogant, unwilling to take criticism, or are rude and unfriendly to other workers, you will quickly be labeled as "immature." It takes too long to pick up the pieces after a bad start, so make every effort to make those beginning weeks and months really count—in the most *positive* way!

You want to make a good early impression, but don't charge ahead trying to impress your boss and your colleagues with all your ideas for overhauling the department. Without fully understanding all of the details, and not yet having a good grasp of the big picture, you will end up looking foolish. Proceed with caution. Acknowledge that there is much you don't know and much for you to learn. Keep your eyes and ears open. Try to learn as much as you can about the organization and your department's role in the organization. You need to have a *thorough* understanding of how things are done before you can begin to make intelligent suggestions for change. Don't make the mistake of believing that after only a quick look at the operation you are ready to offer criticism.

Get to Know the Company Culture

Every firm has its own special personality, a unique set of rules—mostly unspoken—about how to conduct yourself within the company. Most firms seek employees who will fit in and feel at home in their particular culture. Get to know and understand the culture and politics of your new organization. This will help you avoid those embarrassing mistakes that can hinder your advancement.

Remember to pay attention to the way that things are done. Learn the norms by:

- Observing what your co-workers do

- Understanding exactly what is expected of you

- Seeing how people work together and communicate with each other

- Finding ways in which you can comfortably fit in

Have Realistic Expectations

When new workers experience frustration and disappointment on their new job, it is often because they feel their expectations are not being met. Be prepared to have your first job—and even your second or third position—*not* turn out to be everything you imagined it would be. Your first few jobs probably won't be as glamorous, exciting, or important as you had hoped. Skills and teamwork may be more important on the job than you imagined. There is pressure to learn, produce, and meet deadlines, as well as full workdays and even extra hours. Most beginners quickly adjust their expectations to a more realistic level. The work world is different than college. You have probably spent most of your years in school, and the adjustment to a working environment is truly enormous. Aim to be respected by your co-workers and accepted by the organization. *It's your job to make it happen*.

How to Ask for Help
Once You're Hired

Be direct

If you choose *not* to ask for help when you need it, you won't get it and your work will suffer. Keep in mind that every worker, particularly if they are new, needs help from time to time, or another, whether they have a learning disability or not. Asking for help is reasonable, appropriate, and *expected*. Most people are more than willing to help. You'll quickly discover who to avoid and who you can count on.

Be reasonable

Don't expect co-workers to neglect their own work in order to help you do *your* job. Not only is it not fair to them, but they may then focus only on your limitations, especially if it interferes with a work situation. Perhaps you need more training by your supervisor or you need to see more demonstrations of a particular procedure. If you find yourself asking for a lot of help with basic and routine tasks, you are not quite ready to handle that level of the job. Set appropriate limits on the amount of assistance you ask for from co-workers.

Be creative

When you are stumped by a difficult task, try to approach it from another angle. Look at how routines are traditionally handled and aim for a minor change in the procedure, one that might allow you to master it. You and your co-workers, as well as your supervisor, can *all* step back and review the situation to find a way to make it work for you. Of course, this means that you can identify exactly where you are getting bogged down in the task. It will look better if you have thought through several alternate approaches.

Dealing with Difficult Co-Workers

Conflict in the workplace is inevitable. Every new work situation opens up the possibility of new contacts and new learning experiences. But a new job can also bring you into contact with difficult co-workers. In most cases, it makes sense to simply limit your contact with them. In some instances, however, this just isn't possible. The difficult worker might be someone you interact with every day. Unfortunately, that difficult worker could even be your supervisor or manager.

Obviously, you can't change the behavior of another person. Your best bet is to learn to control your own reactions.

- Try not to act in an unprofessional manner by making a scene or really losing your temper. You'll end up looking as bad as the person who provoked you.

- Don't excuse a difficult co-worker's behavior—you really can't pretend that bad manners or discourteous actions are acceptable.

If your encounter a co-worker who seems to delight in intimidating others with tirades and temper tantrums, stay calm and cool. Try not to respond in an explosive manner. Any non-threatening comment that you can make might help defuse the tension, although this is hard to do when you are being at-tacked. You might consider saying:

- "I'd be glad to talk about this issue in a little while, when you've calmed down."

- "Please lower your voice. I am uncomfortable when you shout at me."

- "Slow down a bit. I want to hear what you're saying so I can understand why you are so upset."

Angry people want to be heard and listened to. If you can reassure a raging co-worker that you are willing to listen and try to understand the upsetting issue, some of the fireworks may die down. Try to establish a dialogue to learn more about how to avoid or diffuse other similar situations from surfacing. You can do this and still stand up for yourself.

Performance Reviews

Job performance evaluations are generally used to assess whether you'll be granted a raise or a promotion—or if you will be asked to continue on the job. In mid-sized and large firms, evaluations are fairly standard and you will be told when to expect them. In smaller businesses and family-run operations, raises and reviews are often subject to the whim of the owner. They can happen without much advance notice.

Handled properly, an evaluation serves a valuable function. It's a formal way to let you know exactly how a professional in your field rates your on-the-job performance. Ideally, an evaluation is a candid exchange of information and impressions relating to your performance over a period of time. It is information you need, feedback that lets you know if you are doing things right. When an evaluation reveals areas where you need to improve, you'll want to know exactly what behaviors need to be changed and how to do it.

Let your supervisor or whoever evaluates you know where you feel you could use more guidance and direction. Look at the evaluation as a chance to get the help that you need and an opportunity to strengthen the relationship between you and your boss.

If your company has an annual review policy, don't be timid about asking your supervisor to give you more frequent and informal reviews. These should be "off the record," but the information you get should be viewed as tips to help you stay on track. You will be able to make positive adjustments in your performance without waiting an entire year for the more formal review. It also signals to the management that you are interested in doing the best job possible.

If you and your supervisor agree on a set of goals for you to achieve within a particular time frame, you should ask if you can have it in writing. Otherwise, compose your own memo to your supervisor, keeping a copy for yourself. Simply outline what was discussed. It might read like this:

---

date: _____
TO: Joanne Magli, Art Department Supervisor
FROM: Joan Moriyama, Design Assistant

Thank you for the time you spent with me yesterday reviewing my job performance. I am pleased that you have good feelings about what I have learned so far and my ability to contribute to the department.

As we agreed, I will make every effort to learn Aldus FreeHand and Adobe Illustrator programs by September. I plan to work with Julia Lee during lunch breaks for the next few weeks. She has agreed to spend as much time with me as I need. I feel confident that I will master that goal, as I really enjoy working on the computer.

I will also pay closer attention to my arrival time. I plan on taking an earlier bus in the morning so that I am at my workstation by 9:00 AM.

Working with Your New Boss

Your relationship with your new supervisor or manager will require some special attention. Make sure you get started on the right track!

- Ask for very clear directions about how to approach your new set of duties, and find out what tasks take priority.

- Try to get a solid overview of your department's responsibilities and goals in relation to other units.

- Find out what deadlines have to be met. Are they daily? Weekly? Monthly?

- Be prepared when you spend time with your boss. Have a list of well-thought-out questions or agenda items that you can refer to without wasting time.

- Unless your boss shows some interest in being chatty, get right to the point and don't linger after your questions and concerns have been addressed.

- Never criticize your supervisor to other employees, particularly those from other work units. Remain loyal. Be professional and mature.

- Always let your boss know if you need to leave work early for an unplanned emergency or if you will need additional time on your lunch break. But don't make a habit of this!

- If the department doesn't have a sign-out sheet, let your boss know when you are leaving for a lunch break. That way he or she will be aware of your schedule.

- Show good judgment. Arrive on time. Be ready to stay late if you need to finish important assignments. Always be ready to put in a full day's work.

Keep in mind that supervisors value:

- A positive attitude
- Skills to meet the job requirements
- Good communications skills
- Appropriate dress
- Quality performance
- Productivity
- Dependability
- Assertiveness
- Decision-making ability

- Leadership skills
- Motivation
- Team players

Summary: Getting Off
on the Right Foot

Know your job

- Know the duties and responsibilities
- Know the commitments your employer has made to you
- Know the rules of the company that hired you

Complete your assignments

- Listen carefully to your supervisor's instructions
- Ask questions so that you can do the work properly
- Let your boss know when you've made a mistake so it can be corrected
- Let it be known when you can't finish a project in the time allowed
- Do a good job with *all* the tasks assigned to you, not just those you enjoy
- Be willing to take on extra assignments or work overtime
- Take pride in doing your best

Deal sensibly with authority

- If you believe your supervisor has made a mistake, discuss it calmly
- Talk to co-workers about the best way to deal with your supervisor
- Let your supervisor know the areas that you would like more help with

- If your supervisor is not receptive, talk with the Human Resources department
- Recognize that your supervisor expects you to follow company rules

Use your time efficiently

- Try not to waste time or materials
- Work at a pace that is sensible for you
- Check with your supervisor to see which project needs to be handled first
- Don't socialize with colleagues on office time
- Ask your supervisor if you can do additional projects if all your work is complete
- Explore the possibilities of working in areas you'd like to become more familiar with

Ease into the new work setting

- Relax and do your best
- Don't let your nervousness interfere with your ability to do the job
- Let your supervisor know what areas you are having trouble adapting to
- Avoid being late or absent
- Put in a full day's work each day
- Make advance arrangements with your supervisor when you need to take time off

---

Organize your personal life so that it doesn't interfere with your work!

29

Take Charge of
Your Career

Once you can catch your breath and relax a bit on your new job—enjoy the feeling! But never assume that your career goals will be fulfilled without you taking charge. You alone are responsible for the direction your career path takes.

Nurturing Your Career

Review your career goals periodically to be sure that they are still important to you. It is more than okay for you to change your goals as you mature and gain experience. And it's fine to take detours on your career path and explore interesting areas of the work world that you haven't yet considered. New experiences, as well as new contacts, may open doors that can move you in directions you never dreamed of. Taking risks is fine—as long as you understand the plusses and the minuses of every move.

Keep Learning

You will need to frequently reassess your strengths and weaknesses, and re-examine your values, skills, aptitudes, and interests.

Pay attention to the areas that you need to improve or develop. Decide how you can best improve yourself as a worker. This could mean working on a personal characteristic, such as self-confidence or public speaking, or a more specific work-related issue, such as acquiring leadership skills or mastering a foreign language.

Learn from your present job. You want your first work experience to be as meaningful as possible. This involves being a productive worker for your employer, as well as taking advantage of all the opportunities for growth and development. Keep your eyes and ears open. Volunteer for assignments that offer you exposure to brand new areas of your industry.

Try to profit from your performance reviews. Take seriously how you are evaluated by seasoned professionals in your field. Use that feedback wisely to plan for and cultivate areas that need change or growth.

Enhance your current position. Discuss with your own supervisor or Human Resources contact how you might be able to expand your current job to include new or higher-level duties. Try to be specific about how you could help the company by moving your special skills and expertise into other areas. Make sure you give a thoughtful and well-rehearsed presentation. Think through ahead of time *why* you'd like to expand your current responsibilities. What specifically interests you about the job you'd like to be doing? What qualifications do you have to handle that work? If you feel the firm will benefit from your job performance if it is expanded or changed, specify that too.

You may be told that you are not quite ready for the changes you had in mind. Be prepared for this to happen. It is only a slight setback and eventually you will be ready. Use the time to talk about the types of opportunities that you might prepare for in the near future. Show your enthusiasm and willingness to work towards them, and ask what kinds of training or exposure would improve your chances for consideration.

Keep your networking contacts alive. Don't make the common mistake of forgetting how valuable colleagues and industry contacts can be. The networking process is always less stressful when you are employed, as you aren't focusing on uncovering new job leads.

Continue to attend professional meetings and industry trade shows. Take the initiative of reaching out and meeting new people. Be sure to exchange business cards. Keep in phone contact with others who have been helpful to you in the past. Let them know about your progress at work and remind them of how you have valued their help in the past.

Success Happens

Success on the job is *not* reserved for only a lucky few. You can make it happen for you! Thousands of other young adults with learning disabilities have made it happen for them.

We all know that employers want to hire qualified applicants. By preparing yourself, understanding the job hunting process, and constantly practicing your presentation to make it better for the next time, you too can make success happen for you. It's no accident that some people get job offers or that their career paths move in the right directions. You can make things happen!

The Choice Is Yours

Far too many people find themselves in work situations that they never planned for or gave any thought to. This can result in years of frustration, unhappiness, and disappointment on the job. Don't allow the thousands of hours you will spend at work to be anything but rewarding.

The most satisfying careers don't necessarily follow a straight path. Allow for all the detours you need as you move along. Consider exploring new areas of work—in new fields. Or consider different formats of work—part-time positions, freelance assignments, or volunteer situations. Decide how you can best apply your skills and experiences to various aspects of the industry. Look for opportunities to get additional education and training. And *never* forget yourself in all this. Leave time for your personal growth and development. Family involvement, travel, ongoing education, and relaxation—all of these activities will enhance a thoughtfully planned career. You have the power to make it happen. The choice is yours!

Appendix

Helpful Resources

The following books, agencies, and associations are very helpful resources. Don't limit yourself to these excellent sources of information. Also ask your school or local librarian, as well as any special education counselors and professionals, to help you learn more about the wealth of information and services currently available for people with learning disabilities.

For College Administrators and Faculty

Association on Higher Education & Disability (AHEAD)
P.O. Box 21192
Columbus, OH 43221-0192
(614) 488-4972

Supplies information on technical resources of accommodations.

The Attention Deficit Information Network, Inc.
(AD-IN)
475 Hillside Avenue
Needham, MA 02194
(617) 455-9895

Non-profit volunteer organization that offers support and information to families of children with attention deficit disorders,
and to adults with ADD. The network consists of over 60 national and international chapters.

> Children and Adults with Attention Deficit Disorder
> (CHADD)
> 499 Northwest 70th Avenue, Suite 308
> Plantation, FL 33317
> (305) 587-3700

Non-profit parent-based organization which disseminates information about ADD. There are close to 500 parent-support groups.
The organization publishes a newsletter and a semi-annual magazine.

Financial Aid

> Federal Aid Student Fact Sheet
> U.S. Department of Education
> Office of Student Financial Assistance
> Washington, DC 20202
> (800) 433-3243

This fact sheet describes the six basic federal programs for undergraduate and graduate students and their families.

Internship Resources

Internships provide experience, contacts, and confidence—but
don't expect money! They are a great way to move into a tight job
market. More and more companies, particularly large ones, use
internships as a means of reviewing a candidate's strengths and
determination to succeed. The following books will help you get
started thinking about these wonderful opportunities.

- *Peterson's Internships*. Published by Peterson's Guides.

- *The Princeton Review's Student Access Guide to America's Top 100 Internships*, by Mark Oldman and Samer Hamadeh. Published by Villard Books.
- *A Student's Guide to Volunteering*, by Theresa DiGeronimo. Published by Career Press.
- *Summer Adventures*, by Curtis Casewit. Published by Collier Books.

There are also organizations you can contact for information about internships.

Center for Interim Programs
(617) 547-0980

Inroads (For minority candidates)
(314) 241-7330

Organizations for People with Learning Disabilities

HEATH Resource Center
One DuPont Circle N.W., Suite 800
Washington, DC 20036-1193
(800) 544-3284

HEATH serves as an information exchange of educational and training opportunities for people with disabilities.

Learning Disabilities Association (LDA)
4156 Library Road
Pittsburgh, PA 15234
(412) 341-1515

This national organization is devoted to defining and finding solutions for a broad spectrum of learning disabilities. The LDA provides information and referrals to those searching for publications, support groups, or networking opportunities. You can get a listing of state chapters by calling or writing. The LDA has over 50 state affiliates, with more than 800 local chapters. Members include parents, professionals, and concerned others.

Learning Disabilities Network
72 Sharp Street, Suite A-2
Hingham, MA 02043
(617) 340-5605

This network provides educational and referral services for individuals with learning disabilities and their families, as well as for professionals. It plans conferences, seminars, and workshops. The focus is primarily on the Northeastern region.

National Center for Learning Disabilities (NCLD)
381 Park Avenue South, Suite 1420
New York, NY 10016
(212) 545-7510

This national non-profit organization was established in 1977 to improve the lives of people with learning disabilities. It offers legislative advocacy and educational programs, and strives to raise public awareness and understanding. The NCLD has a referral service and also produces newsletters, a magazine, and a video series.

National Information Center for Children and Youth
With Disabilities
(NICHCY)
P.O. Box 1492
Washington, DC 20013-1492
(800) 695-0285

An information clearinghouse that provides free information on disabilities and disability-related issues. Children and youth to age 22 are the special focus. They will respond to your questions and share information.

National Networker
808 North 82nd Street
Scottsdale, AZ 85257
(602) 941-5112

Newsletter is written by and for adults with learning disabilities, and by concerned others.

Orton Dyslexia Society International
The Chester Building
8600 LaSalle Road
Baltimore, MD 21286-2044
(800) 222-3123

This international, non-profit organization is concerned with dyslexia. The society promotes effective teaching and related clinical strategies; supports and encourages interdisciplinary study and research; and disseminates information through conferences, publications, and volunteer branches staffed by professionals.

Reading for the Blind
The Library of Congress
National Library Service for the Blind & Physically Handicapped
1291 Taylor Street, N.W.
Washington, DC 20452
(202) 287-5100

This cassette tape library is run by a branch of the Library of Congress. They may be willing to provide you with taped texts that are not in their collection. *The federal government considers people with learning disabilities eligible for this service.* To qualify, you need to have documentation that your specific learning disability prevents you from reading easily. Inquire about a free directory of volunteers who produce tape-recorded reading materials. Your local library may have details about this service.

Recording for the Blind (RFB)
20 Roszel Road
Princeton, NJ 08540
(800) 221-4792

A non-profit organization serving people with a print disability—physical impairments such as blindness or a learning disability. The service includes a free, educational library of recorded books and a recording service for new titles (through the post-graduate level). There is a one-time registration fee of $25. You need to document your disability to qualify for service.

Useful Publications for Students with Learning Disabilities

Lovejoy's College Guide for the Learning Disabled, by Charles Straughn. Published by Simon & Schuster.

Profiles over 270 colleges and universities that offer support services for students with learning disabilities.

A National Directory of Four Year Colleges, Two Year Colleges and Post High School Training Programs for Young People with Learning Disabilities. Edited by P.M. Fielding and Dr. J.R. Moss. Published by Partners in Publishing, 1419 West 1st Street, Tulsa, OK 74127.

Lists colleges with programs for students with learning disabilities by state.

Peterson's Colleges with Programs for Students with Learning Disabilities, by Charles Mangrum and Stephen Strichart. Published by Peterson's Guides.

This directory profiles over 1,000 two- and four-year colleges that offer comprehensive programs, as well as special services, for students with learning disabilities.

Standardized Testing

High School Equivalency Test

People with learning disabilities who want to take the high school equivalency exam can get special accommodations and special editions of the test through the General Educational Development (GED) Testing Service. You will need to provide proof of your disability. Special editions include large print and audio-cassette tapes. You can request additional time, distraction-free test rooms, low-glare lighting, and other accommodations. The final test results will not reveal that the test was taken under special conditions. Contact your state's Department of Education for additional details.

College Testing

Students with learning disabilities can get special accommodations and special editions of the two most commonly used admissions tests—the Scholastic Aptitude Test (SAT) and the American College Test (ACT). Arrangements include extended time, readers, cassettes, large type, flexible test dates, distraction-free rooms, marking assistance, and individualized supervision. These requests must be made well in advance of the test date.

The SAT will note that the test was taken under non-standard conditions. The ACT makes no reference to special conditions, unless extended time was granted. You have the option of taking the test either with or without special accommodations.

For more information:

> ATP Services for Handicapped Students
> CN 6400
> Princeton, NJ 08541-6400
>
> The ACT Assessment
> Special Testing Guide Test Administration
> P.O. Box 168
> Iowa City, IA 52543
> (319) 337-1332